S

GUIDE TO THE COMMUNITY CHARGE

BY

MARTIN WARD   JOHN ZEBEDEE

Institute of Housing
9 White Lion Street
London N1 9XJ

SHAC
189a Old Brompton Road
London SW5 0AR

CPAG Ltd.
1–5 Bath Street
London EC1V 9PY

INSTITUTE OF HOUSING

The Institute of Housing is the professional organisation for people working in housing. It stands for ensuring that:

☐ everyone has a decent home to live in at a price they can afford and with secure conditions; and

☐ people who work in housing are well trained, adequately paid and have the tools to do the job.

The Institute has an extensive range of publications and runs a large number of training courses that are open to all. Details of our publications may be obtained from the Publications Officer whilst details about training courses may be obtained from the training section.

SHAC

SHAC opened in 1969 as London's first independent housing aid centre. Its work covers the whole range of housing problems, including homelessness, security of tenure, disrepair and mortgage arrears. SHAC has given advice to over 100,000 households.

SHAC publications and training courses draw on this direct advice-giving experience; it produces a range of advice booklets, publishes research into major housing issues and provides information and training for a wide range of voluntary and statutory organisations.

For further information about SHAC publications, contact the publications office, for details of training courses contact the training unit.

SHAC receives financial support from the Department of the Environment and many other public authorities and private and corporate donors.

CHILD POVERTY ACTION GROUP

CPAG has been leading the fight against family poverty in Britain since its foundation as a national charity in 1965. It runs a national welfare rights resource centre for benefits advisers to ensure that low income families get the welfare benefits to which they are entitled.

Every year it publishes the widely-acclaimed *National Welfare Benefits Handbook* and the *Rights Guide to Non-Means-Tested Benefits*. Other publications include *CPAG's Housing Benefit and Community Charge Benefit Legislation* and pamphlets on poverty, social security, the impact of the Poll Tax etc.

CPAG is also the leader in the field of welfare rights training. The best way of keeping up-to-date with welfare rights and poverty issues is to join CPAG as a member. Members also support CPAG's work for a fairer future for low income families and their children.

For further details of CPAG's publications, training courses and membership schemes, please write to CPAG, 1-5 Bath Street, London EC1V 9PY.

Contents

ACKNOWLEDGEMENTS

We are very grateful for the help given to us in researching and producing this Guide by Bill Bell, Bill Irvine, Jim Read, David Williams and many other colleagues.

Martin Ward and John Zebedee
January 1990

ISBN 0 948857 34 X (SHAC/IOH)
ISBN 0 946744 22 X (CPAG Ltd)

© The Institute of Housing, SHAC and CPAG Limited, 1990

Typeset by Rapid Communications Ltd, London WC1
Printed by WBC (Print) Ltd, Bristol
Bound by W.H. Ware & Sons Ltd, Clevedon, Avon
Production by David Williams Associates, 01-521 4130

Glossary of main terms used in this Guide

Personal community charge

The community charge paid by most individuals (Chapter 2) unless they are exempt (Chapter 3).

Standard community charge

The community charge paid on empty properties, second homes, etc (Chapter 4).

Collective community charge

The community charge paid by the landlords of short-stay hostels, etc (Chapter 5).

Collective contributions

The payments made by the residents of short-stay hostels, etc to their landlords, instead of paying a personal community charge (Chapter 6).

Authority

The term is used in this Guide to apply to any authority which raises the community charge (Chapters 1 and 13).

Community charge register

The details held on all those people liable to pay a community charge (Chapter 8).

Public extract

The part of the register which is available for public inspection (Chapter 9).

Registration officer

The chief finance officer of an authority (assessor in Scotland) whose duty it is to maintain the register and public extract (Chapter 8).

Multiplier

The figure by which the personal community charge is multiplied to work out how much a standard community charge is to be

	(Chapter 4); and also, in Scotland, how much a collective community charge is to be (Chapter 5).
Community charge benefit	The benefit available to people who are liable for a personal community charge or for collective contributions (Chapter 7).
Transitional relief	The help available to some personal community chargepayers (Chapter 7).
Responsible person	Someone whom the registration officer has said must provide information about the residents of a property (Chapter 8).

CHAPTER 1

Introduction

1.1 All adults in England, Wales and Scotland are affected by the community charge (or poll tax). Either they have to pay a charge (or charges) or they have to show that they are exempt. The principles are straightforward, the details anything but. This Guide is designed to enable every reader to find out what he or she needs to know. It covers the questions of interest to administrators and advisers, as well as the general reader. Indeed, it is intended that everyone will find it clear and convenient to use.

1.2 The next few paragraphs provide a broad overview of the community charge, showing which chapter to turn to for further information. There is a summary of the main terms used on page (v), and a full index at the end. The remainder of this chapter covers various background issues, and explains the references which appear in the margins throughout the book.

Overview of the community charge and chapter summary

1.3 The community charge takes over where domestic rates left off. Although domestic rates are now abolished, councils still charge non-domestic rates on shops, offices and other business premises. The community charge and non-domestic rates go principally towards the cost of local services.

1.4 There are 5 kinds of payment under the community charge system:

☐ personal community charge;

☐   standard community charge;
☐   standard community charge contributions (these do not apply in England and Wales, only in Scotland);
☐   collective community charge; and
☐   collective community charge contributions.

THE PERSONAL COMMUNITY CHARGE: CHAPTER 2

1.5 Most people over 18 have to pay a personal community charge to the authority where their only or main home is. This is usually the same for each adult in the area, though transitional rules mean that some people pay less. In a family of two parents and an adult son or daughter, each of the three has to pay a personal community charge. Many students in full-time advanced education only have to pay one fifth of the normal amount.

EXEMPTIONS: CHAPTER 3

1.6 Some people do not have to pay any personal community charge, so long as they can show that they fall into one of the groups laid down by law as exempt. There are a number of such groups, including, e.g., children who stay on at school after their 18th birthday, long-stay hospital patients, and others.

THE STANDARD COMMUNITY CHARGE: CHAPTER 4

1.7 People who own (or in some cases rent) a second home or holiday home usually have to pay a standard community charge to the authority where that home is. This only applies if no-one has his or her only or main home there. The amount may be up to twice the amount of that authority's personal community charge. There is nothing to pay for some kinds of property (e.g. unfurnished property undergoing alteration), and in Scotland a standard community charge-payer can sometimes pass the cost on to a tenant in the form of a standard community charge contribution.

THE COLLECTIVE COMMUNITY CHARGE: CHAPTER 5

1.8 In some hostels and short-stay accommodation it would be difficult for the authority to keep track of the residents, and then charge them all the personal community charge. The authority may therefore decide to make the landlord responsible for a collective community charge on the property.

COLLECTIVE COMMUNITY CHARGE CONTRIBUTIONS: CHAPTER 6

1.9 If the landlord has to pay a collective community charge, he or she in turn collects contributions from most of the residents there, so long as they are over 18. The amount each resident has to pay works out the same as the personal community charge, though it is usually payable for much shorter intervals. There are rules about the landlord's duty to keep residents informed, provide receipts, etc.; and about the residents' duty to pay and right to recover overpayments.

HELP WITH PAYING THE COMMUNITY CHARGE: CHAPTER 7

1.10 Anyone who pays a personal community charge may get help with the cost through the system known as transitional relief. This usually only applies to householders and elderly and disabled non-householders. Anyone who has to pay a personal community charge or collective community charge contribution can claim community charge benefit towards it. However, students who only have to pay one fifth of the personal charge cannot. There are rules about how much benefit each claimant gets and how it is awarded. More detail is given in the companion to this book, *Guide to Housing Benefit and Community Charge Benefit*.

COLLECTION OF INFORMATION: CHAPTER 8

1.11 In order to know who has to pay the community charge, each authority has a registration officer whose job it is to compile a community charge register, and keep it up to date. Various people in various circumstances have to provide information to the registration officer for this purpose, and he or she can also obtain information from a number of other sources.

PROVISION AND INSPECTION OF INFORMATION: CHAPTER 9

1.12 In order to satisfy themselves that the information held about them is correct, chargepayers have the right to find out what information is held on them. Everyone is notified about the information held on the register about them, and may inspect it at any time. The public may also inspect an extract of names and addresses of people who have to pay a charge. Individuals may apply to be left off the public extract if they might otherwise be subject to threats of violence. The general public may also obtain information on properties where the residents have to pay collective community charge contributions. Some other officials have the right to obtain information from the registration officer.

BILLS AND PAYMENTS: CHAPTER 10

1.13 Most people pay their community charge in 10 instalments per year, though there are other possible methods. There are further rules about bills, overpayments, etc. In particular, couples (married or living together as husband and wife) may be called on to pay each other's bills.

PENALTIES AND ENFORCEMENT: CHAPTER 11

1.14 There are various circumstances in which people may have to pay a penalty if they fail to provide information. In Scotland, they may have to pay a surcharge or interest. In England and Wales, landlords responsible for a collective community charge may have to pay a penalty if they fail in their duties towards the authority or their residents. There are also a number of procedures which authorities may use to recover debts from chargepayers. If the authority gets a court order about the debts, the bailiffs may have the power to remove and sell belongings, the person's employer may have to deduct money from his or her pay, or the social security office may deduct money from the person's income support.

APPEALS: CHAPTER 12

1.15 There are a number of grounds on which people may wish to appeal against a decision made about them or about their community charge. There are special procedures for this which may involve a

Valuation and Community Charge Tribunal (in England and Wales) or an appeal to the Sheriff (in Scotland).

FINANCE: CHAPTER 13

1.16 The community charge is raised to pay for the services of district, county, London and metropolitan councils (in England and Wales) and district, island and regional councils (in Scotland). In some cases they raise the community charge themselves. In some cases they raise money via the community charge of another council (e.g. county councils raise money via the district councils' community charge). There are various rules about the setting of the community charge and its relationship with other monies received by authorities (such as revenue support grants from the government, and the operation of the safety net between authorities).

Background

ENGLAND, WALES AND SCOTLAND

EW Act ss 1, 117,118
S Act ss 1,7

1.17 Domestic rates in Scotland were abolished from 1 April 1989, and replaced by the community charge. One year later, from 1 April 1990, domestic rates in England and Wales were abolished, and replaced by the community charge. There are numerous differences of detail between the Scottish system of community charge and that in England and Wales. This Guide covers both systems. In some chapters it has been necessary only to point out the differences as they arise. In others, it has been necessary to have separate sections on the 2 systems.

WATER CHARGES

S Act s 25
sch 5
S SI 1988
No.1538

1.18 In Scotland, the community charge system is mirrored by a community water charge system, and both payments are collected at the same time. This does not apply in England and Wales. For each of the 5 payments listed in para. 1.4 above, there is an equivalent community water charge. A personal, standard or collective community water charge is due unless the property concerned has no domestic water supply, or the water supply is wholly paid for by meter. Collective (or standard) community water charge contributions are due to the landlord, if he or she pays a collective (or standard) community water charge to the authority. Generally, all the rules applying to the community charge in Scotland also apply to the community water charge.

NORTHERN IRELAND

1.19 The Government has no plans to abolish domestic rates in Northern Ireland. This Guide does not therefore apply at all in Northern Ireland.

WHO RAISES THE COMMUNITY CHARGE?

EW Act ss 1, 144

1.20 In England and Wales, the authorities which raise the community charge are known as 'charging authorities'. These are:

- ☐ district councils in England and Wales;
- ☐ London borough councils;
- ☐ the Common Council of the City of London; and
- ☐ the Council of the Isles of Scilly.

S Act s 7 sch 2

1.21 In Scotland, the authorities which raise the community charge are known as 'levying authorities'. These are:

- ☐ islands' councils, whose charges cover their own operations; and
- ☐ regional councils, whose charges cover their own operations and those of district councils.

S Act sch 2

1.22 However, in Scotland, a levying authority may agree with one of the following housing bodies to undertake on its behalf the functions of billing (including levying appeals: para. 12.54), collecting and recovering the community charge and administering community charge benefit:

- ☐ a district council;
- ☐ Scottish Homes;
- ☐ a new town development corporation.

1.23 In this Guide, the term 'authority' is used to cover any of the above, i.e. charging authorities, levying authorities and housing bodies acting on agency for a levying authority.

DUTIES OF AUTHORITIES AND REGISTRATION OFFICERS

1.24 Each authority has a community charge registration officer, who has an independent duty to keep the community charge register up to date. In England and Wales, the registration officer is also the authority's chief finance officer (in Scotland, assessor). In the latter role, he or she will usually be responsible for the other aspects of the community charge: billing, collection, recovery and often community charge benefit. (In Scotland, the registration officer is usually also the electoral registration officer of the authority.) This does not obscure the fact the two (or three) sets of duties are independent, and have been indicated as such in this Guide, by specifying whenever necessary which duties are those of the registration officer and which duties are those of the authority as a whole.

Legal background and references

1.25 The law about the community charge in Scotland is quite separate from that in England and Wales. The two schemes are introduced under different Acts of Parliament. The law in Scotland is introduced by the Abolition of Domestic Rates Etc. (Scotland) Act 1987. The law in England is introduced by the Local Government Finance Act 1988, which also amended the Scottish Act. Both Acts were in turn amended by the Local Government and Housing Act 1989. The Acts are supported by different sets of statutory instruments (which have the force of law) and guidance (which do not). All these are summarised in the tables of references at the end of this chapter.

CHANGES TO THE COMMUNITY CHARGE SCHEMES

1.26 During the course of writing this Guide, various changes have taken place in the operation of the community charge schemes in both England and Wales and in Scotland. The Guide is up to date as the law stood on 22 January 1990.

MARGINAL REFERENCES

1.27 Throughout this book, there are marginal references showing which piece of law covers the matter under discussion. These are designed for further reference, and it is not necessary for the general reader to use them in order to appreciate the community charge schemes.

1.28 The marginal references usually contain the references to English and Welsh law (prefaced by the letters 'EW') followed by the references to Scottish law (prefaced by the letter 'S'). In all cases, references are to the legislation as amended. It is possible to tell what amendments may affect the Act or statutory instrument in question by consulting the tables at the end of this chapter. The following abbreviations are used in the marginal references:

☐ 'EW Act' means the Local Government Finance Act 1988;
☐ 'S Act' means the Abolition of Domestic Rates Etc (Scotland) Act 1987;
☐ 'reg' or 'regs' means the Community Charges (Administration and Enforcement) Regulations SI 1989 No. 438;
☐ all other statutory instruments are referred to by their year and number, e.g. SI 1988 No. 1539: the following tables give their full titles;
☐ 's' or 'ss' refers to the appropriate section(s) of an Act;
☐ 'sch' refers to the appropriate schedule to an Act or statutory instrument.

CROSS-REFERENCES

1.29 Two kinds of cross-references are used. References to 'para.' are to other paragraphs in this Guide where a term or concept is described, or further discussed. References in the format 'PN No.' followed by a number and a paragraph or section number are to the Community Charge Practice Notes, applicable in England and Wales only. These are produced jointly by the Department of the Environment, the Welsh Office and the local authority associations, and are listed below.

TABLES OF REFERENCES

1.30 Tables 1.1 and 1.2 below list all the legislation available at 22 January 1990. Table 1.3 lists the Community Charge Practice Notes referred to in the Guide.

Table 1.1

COMMUNITY CHARGE LEGISLATION:
SCOTLAND

Abbreviation	*Title*
	Acts of Parliament
S Act	The Abolition of Domestic Rates Etc (Scotland) Act 1987 *as amended by* The Local Government Finance Act 1988, the Local Government and Housing Act 1989, SI 1988 No. 1541, SI 1989 No. 63 and SI 1989 No. 2234
	Statutory Instruments
SI 1987 No. 1489	The Abolition of Domestic Rates Etc (Scotland) Act 1987 Commencement Order (S. 110)
SI 1987 No. 2167	The Non-Domestic Rates and Community Charges (Timetable) (Scotland) Regulations (S. 145) *as amended by* SI 1989 No. 2436
SI 1988 No. 631	The Standard and Collective Community Charges (Scotland) Regulations (S. 71) *as amended by* SI 1988 No. 1540, SI 1989 No. 1004, SI 1989 No. 1476 and SI 1989 No. 2437
SI 1988 No. 1456	The Local Government Finance Act 1988 Commencement (Scotland) Order (S. 141)
SI 1988 No. 1477	The Abolition of Domestic Rates (Domestic and Part Residential Subjects) (Scotland) Regulations (S. 143)
SI 1988 No. 1538	The Community Water Charges (Scotland) Regulations (S. 151) *as amended by* SI 1989 No. 2362
SI 1988 No. 1539	The Community Charges (Registration) (Scotland) (No. 2) Regulations (S. 152) *as amended by* SI 1988 No. 1611
SI 1988 No. 1611	The Community Charges (Registration) (Scotland) (No. 2) Amendment Regulations (S. 156)
SI 1988 No. 1880	The Community Charge (Levying, Collection and Payment) (Scotland) Regulations (S. 174)

Continued

Table 1.1, continued

Abbreviation	Title
	Statutory Instruments, 1989
SI 1989 No. 32	The Personal Community Charge (Students) (Scotland) Regulations (S. 1)
SI 1989 No. 63	The Personal Community Charge (Exemptions) (Scotland) Regulations (S. 6)
SI 1989 No. 241	The Abolition of Domestic Rates (Domestic and Part Residential Subjects) (Scotland) Regulations (S. 24)
SI 1989 No. 476	Community Charges (Information Concerning Social Security) (Scotland) Regulations (S. 58)
SI 1989 No. 507	Community Charges (Deductions from Income Support) (Scotland) Regulations (S. 59)
SI 1989 No. 1371	The Community Charges (Cross-Border Information) Regulations
SI 1989 No. 1476	The Standard and Collective Community Charges (Scotland) Amendment (No. 2) Regulations (S. 117)
SI 1989 No. 1477	The Abolition of Domestic Rates (Domestic and Part Residential Subjects) (No. 2) (Scotland) Regulations (S. 118)
SI 1989 No. 2234	The Personal Community Charge (Exemption for the Severely Mentally Impaired) (Scotland) Regulations (S. 147)
SI 1989 No. 2362	The Community Water Charges (Scotland) Amendment Regulations (S. 154)
SI 1989 No. 2436	The Non-Domestic Rates and Community Charges (Timetable) (Scotland) Amendment Regulations (S. 163)
SI 1989 No. 2437	The Standard Community Charge (Scotland) Regulations (S. 164)
	(SIs 1987 No. 2179, 1988 No. 157, 1988 No. 632, 1988 No. 1540, 1988 No. 1541, 1988 No. 1889 and 1989 No. 1004 no longer apply.)

Table 1.2

COMMUNITY CHARGE LEGISLATION:
ENGLAND AND WALES

Abbreviation	*Title*
	Acts of Parliament
EW Act	The Local Government Finance Act 1988 *as amended by* The Local Government and Housing Act 1989, SI 1989 No. 442, SI 1989 No. 1057 and SI 1989 No. 2274
	Statutory Instruments
SI 1989 No. 438	The Community Charges (Administration and Enforcement) Regulations *as amended by* SI 1989 No. 712, SI 1989 No. 1057 and SI 1989 No. 2274
SI 1989 No. 439	The Valuation and Community Charge Tribunals Regulations
SI 1989 No. 440	The Valuation and Community Charge Tribunals (Transfer of Jurisdiction) Regulations
SI 1989 No. 442	The Personal Community Charge (Exemptions) Order
SI 1989 No. 443	The Personal Community Charge (Students) Regulations *as amended by* SI 1989 No. 2274
SI 1989 No. 475	Community Charges (Information Concerning Social Security) Regulations
SI 1989 No. 712	The Community Charges (Administration and Enforcement) (Amendment) Regulations
SI 1989 No. 1057	The Community Charge (Miscellaneous Provisions) Regulations
SI 1989 No. 1371	The Community Charges (Cross-Border Information) Regulations
SI 1989 No. 2274	The Community Charges (Miscellaneous Provisions) (No. 2) Regulations
SI 1990 No. 2	The Personal Community Charge (Relief) (England) Regulations

Table 1.3

**COMMUNITY CHARGE GUIDANCE:
ENGLAND AND WALES**

Abbreviation	*Title*
	Community Charge Practice Notes, 1988
PN No. 1	An Introduction
PN No. 3	The Community Charges Register
PN No. 4	Data Protection and the Community Charge
PN No. 6	The Community Charges Register: Omission of Names from the Public Extract
PN No. 7	Community Charge Appeals
PN No. 8	The Community Charge Canvass
PN No. 9	Sole or Main Residence *as amended by* letter 26.10.89 from T Teehan, DOE
	(PN Nos. 2 and 5 were superseded by PN Nos. 19 and 21 respectively)
	Community Charge Practice Notes, 1989
PN No. 10	Data Protection and the Community Charge
PN No. 11	Billing for the Community Charge
PN No. 12	Collection of the Community Charge
PN No. 13	The Standard Community Charge
PN No. 14	The Collective Community Charge
PN No. 15	Enforcement of the Community Charge
PN No. 16	Joint and Several Liability
PN No. 17	UK Service Personnel *as amended by* letter 28.12.89 from T Teehan, DOE

Continued

Table 1.3, continued

Abbreviation	Title
PN No. 18	Foreign Diplomats and Visiting Forces *as amended by* letters 18.9.89 from J Fejer, DOE; and 26.10.89 and 28.12.89 from T Teehan, DOE
PN No. 19	Exemptions from the Personal Community Charge
PN No. 20	Civil Penalties
PN No. 21	Community Charge Benefit *as amended by* letter 18.9.89 from J Fejer, DOE
PN No. 22	The Collection Fund in England
PN No. 23	Students and the Community Charge
PN No. 25	Transitional Relief Scheme for England (PN No. 24 does not yet exist.)

CHAPTER 2

The personal community charge

2.1 This chapter describes the personal community charge, which most adults have to pay. It covers:

- ☐ who has to pay;
- ☐ the amount of the charge;
- ☐ the reduction for full-time students; and
- ☐ the concept of 'sole or main residence'.

Who has to pay?

EW Act ss 2,12
S Act s 8

2.2 Each person in England, Wales and Scotland has to pay a personal community charge, unless he or she is under 18 or falls into one of the exempt groups described in Chapter 3. The personal charge is due from individuals only, not from companies, organisations, etc. It is payable to the authority in whose area the person lives. If someone has more than one home, the personal charge is only payable in the area where his or her main home is. In some cases, this is not a straightforward issue (paras. 2.32–36). In Scotland, people who pay the personal charge usually also have to pay the personal community water charge (para. 1.18).

MEMBERS OF A HOUSEHOLD

2.3 Each member of a household who fulfils the conditions has to pay a personal charge. For example, in a family composed of a husband and wife with two children aged 17 and 21 and the husband's mother, each would be liable for a personal charge except the 17-year-old (unless any of them were exempt). Rules on 'joint and several liability' mean that if a member of a couple does not pay the personal charge, it may in some circumstances be collected from his or her partner (paras. 10.60 onwards).

The amount of the charge

ANNUAL AMOUNT

2.4 Each authority sets its own personal community charge as an annual amount. In many authorities this is the same for everyone. In other authorities there is a slight difference between the various areas within it (para. 13.33).

EW Act ss 7,12   **2.5** If the chargepayer is liable for a personal charge for the whole
S Act s 8   financial year, the whole annual amount is due.

PART-YEAR AMOUNT

EW Act ss 7,12   **2.6** If the chargepayer is liable for a personal charge for only part
S Act s 8   of a financial year (e.g. because he or she moves into the area, or becomes 18, during the year) the amount is worked out on a daily basis for the appropriate period:

☐ divide the annual amount by the number of days of the financial year (365 or 366); and

☐ multiply the result by the number of days in the financial year on which the chargepayer is liable for the charge. The financial year runs from 1 April to 31 March inclusive. If the chargepayer is liable for the charge for 2 (or more) unconnected periods of the year, the charge for each period is calculated separately.

EW Act ss 7,8   **2.7** When a personal charge is calculated on a daily basis:
S Act s 11A

☐ a day on which the chargepayer starts to be liable for the charge is counted (e.g. the day the chargepayer moves into the area; the day of the chargepayer's 18th birthday);

☐ a day on which the chargepayer ceases to be liable for the charge is not counted (e.g. the day the chargepayer moves out of the area; the day on which the chargepayer starts to be exempt);

☐ a day on which the chargepayer both starts and ceases to be liable for the charge is not counted (e.g. if a chargepayer moves out of the area on the date of his or her 18th birthday).

OTHER FACTORS

2.8 Future changes in the chargepayer's circumstances are not taken into account, so bills sent out at the beginning of the year are always for the whole annual amount, and bills sent out at the beginning of any part-year period are always for the remainder of the financial year. In each case, adjustments are made only when relevant changes actually occur (Chapter 10).

2.9 The total amount due is lower if the chargepayer is a student in full-time advanced education (paras 2.10 onwards) or qualifies for transitional relief or community charge benefit (Chapter 7) or a discount (paras 10.43–44). In almost all cases, the personal charge may be paid by instalments, in which case additional rules apply (Chapter 10).

Examples

AMOUNT OF PERSONAL COMMUNITY CHARGE

On 1 April 1990, a man has his sole residence in the area of an authority whose personal community charge is £300. He is neither exempt nor a student in full-time advanced education.

His personal charge is calculated on the assumption that his circumstances will not change for the whole financial year. He receives a bill showing the annual amount of £300.

On 13 June 1990 the man in the above example moves to another part of the country, and a woman moves in to his home. She is neither exempt nor a student in full-time advanced education.

The man is liable for the charge up to and including the day before he leaves. From 1 April 1990 to 12 June 1990 inclusive there are 73 days. He is liable for only $^{73}/_{365}$ of the personal charge of £300, which equals £60. The authority adjusts his account accordingly.

The woman's bill is calculated on the assumption that her circumstances will not change. She has to pay a personal charge calculated on a daily basis including the day she moves in. From 13 June 1990 to 31 March 1991 inclusive there are 292 days. She receives a bill for $^{292}/_{365}$ of the personal charge of £300, which equals £240.

The reduction for students in full-time advanced education

EW Act s 13
S Act s 8

2.10 A student in full-time advanced education has to pay only 20 per cent (one fifth) of the personal community charge. This is payable to the authority in whose area the student's term-time address is. This student reduction only applies if all the following conditions are fulfilled:

☐   the course is at a relevant educational establishment;

☐   the student is attending the course;
☐   the course is full-time; and
☐   the student has a certificate from the establishment.

EDUCATIONAL ESTABLISHMENTS

EW SI 1989
No.443
S SI 1989
No.32

2.11 The reduction only applies for courses at relevant educational establishments. These include universities, polytechnics, colleges of education, theological colleges and other institutions providing a similar level of education; and also in certain cases nursing schools (para. 2.22). It does not include further (as opposed to advanced) education (para. 3.11).

ATTENDANCE ON THE COURSE

EW SI 1989
No.443
S SI 1989
No.32

2.12 The student must be enrolled with and attending the establishment in order to qualify for the reduction. The reduction applies for the whole of the course, including the day it begins and the day it ends, and including any short and long (e.g. summer) vacations within that period. It does not apply after the student has completed or abandoned the course, or is no longer permitted by the establishment to attend it. Nor does it apply during any period between two different courses (e.g. during the summer holiday between an undergraduate and post-graduate course).

2.13 The reduction also does not apply before a student begins a course. For example, someone who leaves school in July may not be liable for a personal charge until the first Monday in September (because of the exemption for dependents for whom someone receives child benefit: para 3.9). If she takes up a university course in early October, she will have to pay a personal community charge calculated at the full rate for the period (approximately a month) between early September and early October and then at 20 per cent of the full rate for the remainder of the financial year.

FULL-TIME COURSES

2.14 A course of education is full-time if:

☐ it is for at least one academic year of the establishment, or at least one calendar year;

☐ the students are normally required to attend (at the establishment or elsewhere) for at least 24 weeks in that year; and

☐ during those weeks, the nature of the course would normally require an average of at least 21 hours' study or tuition. This may include work experience relevant to the course.

2.15 In England and Wales the rules include further detail. First, a course where (throughout its length) work experience would normally exceed other periods of study or tuition does not count as full-time. Second, if a course begins part way through the ordinary academic year, the averaging described above is calculated over each year beginning with the first day of the term in which the course begins and, in following years, beginning with the first day of the equivalent term. If the establishment does not have academic years, the averaging is calculated over each calendar year, beginning with the first day of the course and, in following years, beginning with the anniversary of that day. It is not necessary to satisfy the averaging rules in any part year at the end of a course.

THE STUDENT CERTIFICATE

2.16 It is one of the conditions for qualifying for the reduction that the student has a certificate from his or her educational establishment. The format of the certificate and further details are discussed in para. 8.36. This means that in most cases the decision about who qualifies for the student reduction is made by the educational establishment concerned, since registration officers usually assume that possession of a certificate is sufficient evidence that the student fulfils the other conditions. However, the practice note, *Students and the Community Charge*, (PN No. 23, section 3) points out that possession of a certificate is not an automatic ticket to the student reduction: there may be cases where a registration officer is not satisfied that the person satisfies the other conditions even though he or she holds a certificate. On the other hand, it is not necessary for a registration officer to inspect a certificate (if satisfied on other evidence that the person qualifies as a student), though he or she may insist on this.

WHICH AUTHORITY DOES THE STUDENT PAY TO?

EW Act s 2
S Act s 8

2.17 A student who qualifies for a reduction is treated as having sole or main residence at his or her current term-time address, and is therefore liable to pay the reduced personal charge to the authority where that address is. This overrides any other considerations in relation to the student's sole or main residence, and applies throughout the time when the student fulfils the conditions described above – including both short and long (e.g. summer) vacations.

EW Act s 2

2.18 In England and Wales, 2 further rules are provided about this (and Scottish registration officers may well take a similar approach). They apply when a student has no current term-time address, and continue to apply until he or she finds a current term-time address:

☐ a student with no current term-time address (e.g. because he or she has given it up during the summer holidays) continues to be treated as living at his or her most recent term-time address; and

☐ a student with neither current nor former term-time address (e.g. a first year who has not yet found student accommodation, or delays taking up student accommodation because of sickness) is treated as living at whatever his or her sole or main residence is under the ordinary rules (paras 2.23 onwards).

OVERSEAS STUDENTS

2.19 The practice note points out (PN No. 23, paras. 7.3–5) that a full-time student from overseas cannot be treated as having sole or main residence overseas (and therefore wholly exempt from a personal charge), because the above rules override any other consideration. But this does not apply to a part-time student (or a student who did not fulfil any other of the conditions), nor to the partner of a full-time student, nor necessarily in Scotland.

STUDENTS STUDYING OUTSIDE GREAT BRITAIN

2.20 A full-time student who spends a year abroad does have a current term-time address abroad, and therefore the student rules on sole or main residence coincide with the ordinary rules: the student is not liable for any personal community charge. Similarly, a full-time student whose educational establishment (and term-time address) is in Northern Ireland, does not pay any personal community charge (para. 3.14).

NURSING EDUCATION

EW SI 1989
No.443
S Act s 8
S SI 1989
No.32

2.21 A student who fulfils the general conditions described here, qualifies for the student reduction, regardless of whether he or she is studying nursing or some other subject. For example, a student studying nursing at a university or polytechnic may well fulfil the conditions. However, a student nurse undergoing training at a hospital or some similar establishment does not qualify for the reduction.

2.22 The exception is that students undertaking the new 'Project 2000' training courses do qualify for the reduction. This currently applies in some 13 nursing schools in England, and will apply in all nursing schools in Wales from Autumn 1991. The colleges concerned provide student certificates in the same way as other educational establishments do.

Sole or main residence

EW Act s 2(1)
S Act s 8(1)

2.23 The personal community charge is payable to the authority in whose area the person has his or her 'sole or main residence'. This is usually a straightforward question for people with only one home. For people with more than one home, and those who move around frequently, it may be more complicated. The need to decide where someone's sole or main residence is, may arise:

☐   as between different authorities, in order to decide which authority the person pays a personal charge to; or

☐   as between areas within an authority, if the personal charge varies between them (para. 13.33); or

☐   as between different kinds of accommodation, where sole or main residence in one of them would mean that the person concerned was exempt from a personal charge.

2.24 The practice note, *Sole or Main Residence*, (PN No. 9), recognises that 'the concept of sole or main residence is . . . crucial to the structure of the new system'. In most cases, the concept is not defined in law. It is a matter for the registration officer to decide, and may be appealed against (Chapter 12). Special rules apply for students in full-time advanced education (paras 2.10 onwards). The following paragraphs deal first with the other cases where a particular rule exists, and then with general issues.

TYPES OF ACCOMMODATION

EW Act s 2   **2.25** The fact that someone does not live in a building (i.e. a fixed structure) is irrelevant in deciding where his or her sole or main residence is. So there is nothing to stop a person being treated as having sole or main residence in a caravan, mobile home, houseboat, bed and breakfast hotel, residential hotel, hospital, nursing home, tent, etc – though in some of these examples, the person would be exempt from a personal charge (Chapter 3).

NO PERMANENT ADDRESS

EW Act s 31   **2.26** Someone with no fixed abode is treated as having sole or main
S Act sch 1A   residence in the place where he or she is at the time. This applies to someone sleeping rough (who is, however, exempt: para. 3.29) and to someone who moves from address to address with no fixed base. In other words, someone with no accommodation anywhere else is regarded as resident in accommodation where he or she is staying temporarily.

PRISONERS

EW Act ss 2,31   **2.27** Prisoners and others detained in legal custody are never treated as having sole or main residence in the prison, etc, except when they have no fixed abode elsewhere. Most prisoners are, however, exempt (para. 3.35), and so the question does not arise. This rule does not apply in Scotland, where the question of sole or main residence is left open.

GENERAL CASES

2.28 In other cases, the concept of 'sole or main residence' is not defined in law, and therefore takes its ordinary English meaning. The practice note refers (PN No. 9, paras. 2.3–7) to the Oxford English Dictionary definition of 'reside', accepted in other parts of the law, as meaning 'to dwell permanently or for a considerable time, to have one's settled or usual abode, to live in or at a particular place'. It should be emphasised, however, that the question of permanence is not relevant in the case of someone with no fixed abode (para. 2.26).

2.29 It is clear that it is not relevant whether someone is entitled in law to be in a particular place. For example, a squatter may well have sole or main residence in his or her squat. Similarly, someone who has stayed on in rented accommodation after a court order has been made requiring him or her to leave, usually continues to have sole or main residence there. It is also clear that if unrelated law (e.g. electoral law) counts someone as resident in accommodation, this does not necessarily mean that this is the case for community charge law – and vice versa.

CHANGES OF RESIDENCE

2.30 On the day when someone moves home permanently, his or her sole or main residence changes. In fact, he or she has to pay a personal charge only to the authority whose area he or she moves into on that day; and not in the area he or she leaves or passes through (para. 2.7). More difficult questions are addressed in the following examples (and see also PN No. 9, paras. 3.16–17).

2.31 If someone moves temporarily, his or her sole or main residence does not necessarily change (unless he or she has no permanent base: para. 2.26). For example, a short holiday does not change someone's sole or main residence, whereas a long stay with relatives might well do so. It should be noted that the words 'short' and 'long' in this context have no legal definition, but can only be used loosely. Each case must be looked at individually by the registration officer making the decision.

Examples

SOLE OR MAIN RESIDENCE

A woman owns a house in the area of authority A and pays her personal charge there. She sells her house and buys a new one in the area of authority C, but cannot move in at once. In the mean time she stays with relatives in the area of authority B.

There are 4 possible solutions:

(a)   Her sole or main residence remains in area A until the day she moves into the house in area C, at which point it changes to being in area C.

(b)   Her sole or main residence changes to being in area C on the day after she moves out of area A.

(c)   Her sole or main residence changes to being in area B when she moves in there, and then to area C when she moves in there.

(d)   Her sole or main residence remains in area A until some point during her stay in area B, when it changes to being in area C.

A man goes into an NHS hospital for an unpredictable amount of time. Some time later, his consultant tells him it will be a long stay, and he informs the registration officer of this immediately. People who are solely or mainly resident in an NHS hospital are exempt (para. 3.15).

The recommended solution is in (a) below – but authorities may adopt others such as (b), and should be challenged if they do:

(a)   On the day the registration officer is informed, she treats his sole or main residence as being in the hospital, and backdates this to the day he was admitted.

(b)   On the day the registration officer is informed, she treats his sole or main residence as being in the hospital, but refuses to backdate this to the day he was admitted.

MORE THAN ONE HOME

2.32 No-one can have more than one 'sole or main residence' at any one time. An ordinary holiday home (whether in this country or abroad) presents no difficulty: it is unlikely to be the person's sole or main residence. But there are more difficult cases where 2 ordinary homes are occupied at different times of the year, or perhaps by different members of the family.

2.33 In making a decision between more than one home, any relevant factor must be taken into account. The practice note suggests (PN No. 9, paras. 3.5–13) that the most common are likely to be:

☐   how much time is spent in each home;
☐   where the members of the household work;
☐   where children go to school;
☐   an employer's requirements on an employee to occupy tied accommodation and/or to maintain accommodation apart from that tied accommodation;
☐   where the members of the household keep their possessions; and
☐   where appropriate, the views of the chargepayers themselves.

2.34 The practice note emphasises (PN No. 9, para. 3.4) that the question is not to be decided only in terms of the amount of time spent in each home (though in practice, it seems likely that this will very often form the basis for many decisions), and that registration officers should not wait until the end of the year to look back and see how long someone spent in each of his or her homes. The above factors may lead to different conclusions in different cases.

2.35 In particular, 'it should not be assumed that the arrangement least beneficial to [the chargepayer] must inevitably be the correct one' (PN No. 9, para. 3.7). For example, if the members of a couple (or family) actually have their sole or main residence in different homes, the fact that they may therefore avoid paying a standard community charge on one of them is irrelevant.

2.36 In some of these cases, the registration officers from different authorities may need to settle between them which is the sole or main residence of the chargepayer. Failing this a chargepayer registered as liable for a personal charge in 2 or more registers is liable to pay both unless he or she appeals against one or other entry. Once the appeal is made, special provisions apply for ensuring that he or she pays only one personal charge at a time (para. 12.6).

VISITORS FROM (AND TO) OVERSEAS

2.37 The interpretation of sole or main residence may be particularly difficult for visitors from overseas. At one extreme, a visitor who spends a short period in Great Britain, but retains a home abroad, does not have sole or main residence here (and so is not liable for a personal charge). At the other extreme, a visitor spending a long period here, who has given up accommodation abroad, may well have sole or main residence here (and so be liable for a personal charge). In between, there are several grey areas. (For students from overseas there are special rules: para. 2.19.) A similar range of possibilities arises for people who spend time outside Great Britain. 'Tax exiles' often also succeed in being 'personal community charge exiles'.

FORCES PERSONNEL AND MERCHANT SEAGOERS

2.38 The practice notes describe the general agreement reached by registration officers in Scotland on sole or main residence for forces personnel, and suggest that the same approach is adopted in England and Wales and extended to merchant seamen and seawomen (PN No. 17, section 4 and amendment; PN No. 9, amendment). This is not binding, and should be departed from in appropriate individual cases:

☐ for single non-seagoing personnel (regardless of whether they are householders), there is a residence limit of 61 days, up to which a change of posting does not constitute a change of sole or main residence, but beyond which it does;

☐ for married non-seagoing personnel, there is a residence limit of 6 months, up to which a posting away from their home address does not constitute a change of sole or main residence, but beyond which it does;

☐ for single seagoing personnel who are not householders, sole or main residence does not arise except in the case of a stay on shore of more than 61 days;

☐ for single seagoing personnel who are householders, and for married seagoing personnel, sole or main residence remains at their home address unless they are continuously absent (at sea or elsewhere) for more than 6 months.

ACCOMMODATION STRADDLING BOUNDARIES

EW Act ss 2, 12,31   **2.39** If someone's sole or main residence straddles the boundary of two or more areas, the accommodation is treated as being in the area where the greater or greatest part is. This applies both between authorities and (where appropriate) within them. This and the following rules do not have equivalents in Scotland (though similar provisions are likely to apply in practice).

EW regs 53,54   **2.40** Where the greater or greatest part is, is decided by measuring:

☐ the external floor area, in the case of a caravan;

☐ the enclosed volume, in the case of a houseboat;

☐ the external area of the lowest floor, for any other property which is wholly above ground;

☐ the internal area of the lowest floor, for any other property which is below ground;

☐ the area of the ground-level cross section measured externally, for any other property.

EW regs 54,56   **2.41** In each of the above cases, only the main structure is measured, and not any separate structure (e.g. an outhouse or garage). If the accommodation is divided equally between authorities, they must come to an agreement about where it is to be treated as being. If they cannot agree, the decision is made by lot. If the accommodation is divided equally between parts of the same authority, it is up to the authority to decide in which part it is to be treated as being.

CHAPTER 3

Exemptions

3.1 This chapter explains who is exempt from paying the personal community charge described in Chapter 2 and the collective community charge contributions described in Chapter 6. It covers:

- ☐ an overview of the exemptions;
- ☐ how to gain exemption;
- ☐ backdating exemptions; and
- ☐ a description of each exemption in detail.

Overview

EW Act s 2
S Act s 8

3.2 A person is not liable to pay a personal community charge on any day when he or she is exempt, i.e. if he or she fulfils any of the conditions for exemption described below. The exempt groups are summarised in broad terms in the following table (3.1). There is no provision for authorities to offer exemption to anyone else.

Table 3.1

PERSONAL COMMUNITY CHARGE: SUMMARY OF EXEMPT GROUPS

In most cases there are further conditions described in the text

☐ Dependent children aged 18 or over (as well as everyone under 18)
☐ Students under 20 in further education
☐ Students in full-time advanced education whose term-time address is in Northern Ireland
☐ Long-term hospital patients
☐ Residents in nursing homes and residential care homes
☐ Residents in certain hostels
☐ Residents in women's refuges (Scotland only)
☐ Residents in night shelters
☐ People with no fixed abode
☐ People who are 'severely mentally impaired'
☐ Low-paid full-time residential care workers
☐ Prisoners and other people in detention
☐ Members of religious communities
☐ Visiting armed forces, diplomats, etc
☐ Some residents on Crown land
☐ People who pay collective community charge contributions

EW Act s 11   **3.3** Similarly, a person who lives in accommodation where the
S Act s 11   landlord pays a collective community charge does not have to pay
contributions to the landlord if he or she is exempt on any day.
The exempt groups in these cases are almost exactly identical with
those applying for personal charges: the differences are summarised
as they arise.

3.4 A person who is exempt from paying a personal charge (or
contributions) still has to pay any standard or collective community
charge for which he or she is liable. However, the rules on standard
charges provide relief for some people exempt from a personal
community charge (e.g. for hospital patients and some residents in
homes or hostels). These are referred to below.

Gaining exemption

3.5 Entitlement to exemption is automatic, so long as the conditions for it are fulfilled. Most authorities indicate the conditions for exemptions to their personal chargepayers – when they are carrying out a canvass, or when they write to chargepayers about their register entries, or in their general publicity. Nonetheless, it is usually necessary for chargepayers to inform the registration officer that they are or may be exempt, and registration officers may request supporting evidence. Chargepayers may appeal if they are not granted exemption (Chapter 12).

3.6 There is no formal procedure for gaining exemption from paying contributions to a landlord. A resident who experiences difficulty with this could ask the registration officer of the authority concerned to confirm his or her exempt status with the landlord, or contact an advice agency or the council's tenancy relations officer. It may also be possible as a last resort to ask the courts to intervene. If a landlord attempts to recover unpaid contributions in court from an exempt resident, the resident should seek representation, and ensure that his or her representative draws the position clearly to the court's attention.

Backdating exemptions

3.7 Any exemption from a personal community charge can be backdated for up to 2 years (paras 8.14 onwards). There is no requirement on chargepayers to give a reason for the delay in requesting exemption. Backdating is automatic, not discretionary, so long as the conditions for it applied during the backdated period. Nor is there any requirement that the backdated period must be recent (so long as it within the past 2 years) or even continuous. Therefore, no-one who should have been exempt at any time since the introduction of the community charge scheme need lose out, so long as the registration officer is informed by the scheme's second anniversary (1 April 1992 in England and Wales, 1 April 1991 in Scotland). When backdated exemption is granted, any personal charge paid during that period is repayable.

3.8 It is also possible to recover contributions from a landlord for a period when a resident should have been exempt – if necessary in court (paras 6.29–32). In Scotland, such contributions can be recovered only on request (i.e. it is not automatic) and exemption can only be backdated up to 3 months prior to the date of the request. In England and Wales, there is no special procedure, and there appears to be no time limit on backdating.

The exemptions in detail

DEPENDENT CHILDREN

EW Act sch 1
para 5
S Act sch 1A
para 5

3.9 Children do not have pay the personal community charge. This is automatic until their 18th birthday. After that they are only exempt if a parent or other guardian receives child benefit for them, or could receive it if he or she claimed (or if para. 3.11 applies).

3.10 In other words, a child is exempt if he or she is still at school and then for a period after leaving school. Though child benefit is not payable for any week the child is in full-time work, he or she is still exempt until the week of the appropriate terminal date or his or her 19th birthday – whichever comes first. The terminal dates are given below along with the extension period for some children who cannot get YTS places:

- [ ] for summer term school leavers, the first Monday in September (the last Monday in December in extension cases);
- [ ] for autumn term school leavers, the first Monday in January (12 weeks later in extension cases); or
- [ ] for spring term school leavers, the first Monday after Easter Monday (12 weeks later in extension cases).

STUDENTS IN FURTHER EDUCATION

EW Act sch 1
para 6A
S Act sch 1A
para 6A

3.11 Students in further education (e.g. studying A levels or similar level courses at a school or further education college) are exempt from paying the personal community charge until their 20th birthday. In many cases, this exemption immediately follows on from the exemption described above. The course must include an average of 12 hours or more of teaching per week. However, the exemption does not apply if the student is sponsored by an employer in preparation for or during employment, or in association with a YTS scheme. It also does not apply for collective community charge contributions.

3.12 This exemption was introduced by the Local Government and Housing Act 1989 (passed in November 1989). Further education (where the students are exempt) is, in most cases, different from full-time advanced education (where the students pay 20 per cent of the personal charge: paras 2.10 onwards). However, at the time of writing, regulations have not been made detailing exactly which courses (at which kinds of educational establishment) constitute further education for the purposes of this exemption.

LGHA sch 5
paras 14,79

3.13 In Scotland, this new exemption has retrospective effect. Students in further education who have been paying personal charges are entitled to repayment for any period (since 1 April 1989) when they should have been exempt.

STUDENTS WHOSE TERM-TIME ADDRESS IS IN NORTHERN IRELAND

EW Act sch 1
para 6
S Act sch 1A
para 6
S SI 1989
No.63

3.14 Although there is no community charge in Northern Ireland, students there are not expected to pay a personal community charge if they spend time in England, Wales or Scotland (whether during vacations or term-time). The exemption applies to any full-time student in advanced education whose term-time address is in Northern Ireland. The definitions are the same as in paras 2.10 onwards. This exemption does not apply for collective community charge contributions.

HOSPITAL PATIENTS

EW Act sch 1
para 8
S Act sch 1A
para 8

3.15 This exemption applies to any patient who has sole or main residence in any NHS hospital (but not patients in hospitals which are privately maintained). The exemption automatically applies if the patient has no other accommodation. Otherwise, it usually only applies to long-stay patients, since someone who goes into hospital for a brief period still has sole or main residence in his or her ordinary home.

3.16 The question of whether someone's sole or main residence is in hospital or elsewhere may be complicated. The general provisions on sole or main residence apply (paras 2.23 onwards). A particular difficulty arises for someone who goes into hospital for an unpredictable amount of time, if it transpires (at some later date) that the stay is to be long-term. In such a case, there is nothing to stop the registration officer backdating exemption to the date of admission (para. 3.7), and this is the solution recommended here. In practice, the approach to these cases is likely to vary from area to area, and chargepayers are encouraged to appeal against harsh decisions (Chapter 12).

3.17 The practice note, *Exemptions from the Personal Community Charge (2)*, (PN No. 19, para. 11.3) misleadingly draws attention to the rule whereby entitlement to housing benefit ends after 52 weeks in hospital, commenting that 'it will be possible . . . for a person to become solely or mainly resident in a hospital earlier than this, though . . . unusual'. There is no legal justification whatsoever for adopting a 52 week limit. Indeed, the comment would be accurate only if the words 'though unusual' were replaced by 'indeed usual'. Rules on sole or main residence are far more responsive to the facts of a case than the practice note implies. The only justification for adopting even a short limit (say 6 weeks – the period after which most social security benefits reduce for people in hospital) is that it provides a reminder that by then all the facts of the case should be properly evaluated.

3.18 Someone who is exempt from a personal community charge because of being in an NHS hospital is also exempt from paying a standard charge on his or her previous home (para. 4.29). This is automatic for the first 52 weeks in hospital (a point further undermining the comment from the practice note quoted above); after that it is at the authority's discretion.

RESIDENTS IN NURSING HOMES AND RESIDENTIAL CARE HOMES

EW Act sch 1 para 9
EW SI 1989 No.442
S Act sch 1A para 9

3.19 This exemption applies to anyone who has sole or main residence in a nursing home or residential care home, and receives care or treatment or both there (i.e. resident staff are not exempt). It applies to:

☐ residential care homes requiring registration with the social services or social work department, or which are exempt from registration;

☐ nursing homes and mental nursing homes (which may be known as private hospitals in Scotland) requiring registration with the health authority;

☐   residential accommodation run by the NHS, a health authority, a government department, a local authority, Abbeyfield Homes, or some other body set up under an Act of Parliament or Royal Charter.

3.20 Confirmation that accommodation is exempt under these rules usually depends on obtaining proof that the accommodation is registered or that it is run by one of the bodies or organisations mentioned above. Residential care homes with 3 beds or less are exempt from registration, and so registration officers may need to be satisfied that they qualify as such. In order to do so, personal care must be provided, rather than simply board and lodging. This is defined in the Registered Homes Act 1984 as 'care which includes assistance with bodily functions where such assistance is required', e.g. help with washing, dressing, toilet needs, and the administration of medicine. The practice note (PN No. 19, paras 12.9–13) provides further advice, and suggests that registration officers might wish to use a test developed for income support purposes, which presumes that a residential care home should provide unrestricted access to the residents at all times, and have at least 2 experienced staff, with at least one on duty throughout the day and at least one on call throughout the night.

3.21 The points on sole or main residence, and on exemption from a standard community charge, apply here in the same way as for hospital patients (paras 3.16–18).

RESIDENTS IN CERTAIN HOSTELS

EW Act sch 1
para 9
EW SI 1989
No.442
S Act sch 1A
para 9

3.22 This exemption applies to anyone who has sole or main residence in any Home Office approved probation hostel or bail hostel, or in some other hostel which provides personal care and fulfils the further conditions described below. A typical example might be a hospice for the terminally ill.

3.23 In England and Wales, the exemption only applies (except in the case of bail and probation hostels) for hostels and similar establishments where:

☐   the accommodation is mainly not self-contained; and
☐   most of the residents require and are provided with personal care for old age, disablement, past or present alchohol or drug dependence or past or present mental disorder.

3.24 In Scotland, the exemption only applies (except in the case of bail and probation hostels) for hostels and similar establishments which:

☐ are run by a registered housing association, voluntary organisation or other publicly-funded, non-commercial organisation; and

☐ exist to provide board combined with personal care or support (such as the provision of appropriate help with physical and social needs, or counselling or other help as part of a planned programme).

3.25 It is up to the registration officer to decide whether a hostel fulfils these conditions, and residents may appeal. The points on sole or main residence, and on exemption from a standard community charge, apply here in the same way as for hospital patients (paras 3.16–18).

WOMEN'S REFUGES, ETC

S Act sch 1A
para 12
S SI 1989
No.1477

3.26 In Scotland only, anyone whose sole or main residence is in non-domestic property is exempt. Since women's refuges in Scotland are always treated as non-domestic property, any woman whose sole or main residence is in a refuge is exempt. This automatically applies if she no longer has any alternative accommodation. If the registration officer continues to regard her as solely or mainly resident in her former home (and therefore not exempt), she should argue that that cannot be her sole or main residence because she cannot safely return there and, if necessary, appeal (Chapter 12). In England and Wales, there is no equivalent to these rules. Women whose sole or main residence is in a women's refuge have to pay a personal charge or (if the hostel is so designated by the authority) collective community charge contributions.

NIGHT SHELTERS

EW Act sch 1
para 13
EW reg 58

3.27 In England and Wales, this exemption applies to anyone staying in a night shelter, or a similar hostel or other building where:

☐ the accommodation is mainly not self-contained;

☐ most of the residents have no fixed abode and no settled way of life; and

☐ the residents are granted licences rather than tenancies.

3.28 The exemption therefore covers ordinary night shelters, and also churches and other buildings used for temporary accommodation by organisations such as Crisis at Christmas. The length of the resident's stay is irrelevant, so long as the above conditions are fulfilled. The Secretary of State has the power to make a similar exemption in Scotland, but has not done so at the time of writing. Therefore, the exemption applies in Scotland only if the building concerned is subject to non-domestic rates (para. 3.26).

PEOPLE WITH NO FIXED ABODE

EW Act s 31
sch 1 para 14
S Act sch 1A
para 13

3.29 This exemption applies to anyone who has no fixed abode. However, it does not apply if the person ends his or her day in a building (including a chalet or a hut), a caravan, or a houseboat. It therefore only applies for people sleeping rough – or in a tent, car, railway carriage, etc. It does not, in theory apply to someone who usually has no fixed abode but spends a night in a hut or a disused building – though in practice it is unlikely that he or she will receive a personal community charge bill for one day.

PEOPLE WHO ARE 'SEVERELY MENTALLY IMPAIRED'

EW Act sch 1
para 4
EW SI 1989
No.442
S Act sch 1A
para 4
S SI 1989
No.63

3.30 In order to qualify for this exemption, a person must fulfil 3 conditions. They are that the person:

☐ 'has severe impairment of [his or her] intelligence and social functioning from whatever cause';

☐ has a doctor's certificate to this effect; and

☐ is entitled to invalidity pension, severe disablement allowance, unemployability supplement or allowance, attendance allowance, constant attendance allowance or an increase for attendance in his or her disablement pension. This includes cases where the person is entitled to one of those benefits, but receives some other benefit because of the rules on overlapping social security benefits.

3.31 The rules in Scotland until 29 December 1989 extended the third condition above to anyone over pensionable age (60 for a woman, 65 for a man) but excluded recipients of attendance allowances. People who then qualified as exempt continue to do so. The first condition above was at that time stricter, applying only to those suffering mental impairment from youth or as a result of brain damage. People who now qualify for exemption following the widening of this rule should have this backdated as far as appropriate. The Scottish rules were also originally planned for England and Wales: at the time of writing, amendments are still required to bring the law in England and Wales into line with the provisions outlined above, and may differ in detail.

3.32 The practice note (PN No. 19, paras. 7.6–11) suggests that registration officers should first confirm that the potentially exempt chargepayer fulfils the third of the conditions mentioned above, and then obtain permission to contact his or her doctor direct. Registration officers are provided with standard forms in triplicate, for the doctor to complete; one copy for the doctor to retain, one copy for the registration officer to retain, and one for the registration officer to send to the chargepayer with the notification of the decision about exemption. Doctors provide this service free. The nature of this exemption is that, once fulfilled, it is likely to last for life. The copy of the doctor's certificate kept by the exempt person may therefore be used should he or she move to another area.

RESIDENTIAL CARE WORKERS

EW Act sch 1
para 10
EW reg 63
S Act sch 1A
para 10
S SI 1989
No.63

3.33 This exemption only applies if all the following conditions are fulfilled:

☐ the carer is employed to provide care or support (or both) to another person or persons;

☐ the contract of employment requires at least 24 hours per week to be spent as a carer;

☐ the pay from that employment is £25 per week or less (excluding payment in kind such as the provision of free accommodation);

☐ the carer resides in premises provided by the employer for the purpose of the employment; and

☐ the employer is:
   – a solely charitable organisation such as Community Service Volunteers; or
   – the person (or at least one of the persons) for whom the care or support is provided, but only if he or she was introduced to the carer by a solely charitable organisation; or
   – in Scotland only, some other person or body introduced to the carer by a solely charitable organisation; or
   – in England and Wales only, a local authority, a government department or any other public authority.

3.34 The practice note (PN No. 19, para. 13.4) suggests that this is unlikely to include cases where the carer is a relative or friend of the person cared for, since it would be necessary for an introduction to have been made by a charitable body and for there to be contract of employment.

PRISONERS AND OTHER PEOPLE IN DETENTION

EW Act sch 1
paras 1,8,9
EW SI 1989
No.442
S Act sch 1A
para 1
S SI 1989
No.63

3.35 This exemption applies for almost all forms of custodial detention. It applies to anyone who is detained:

☐ in a prison, hospital, or other place as a result of a decision of any UK court. This includes periods on remand regardless of the outcome of the case;

☐ under the deportation provisions in the Immigration Act 1971;

☐ under the Repatriation of Prisoners Act 1984;

☐ under the provisions of the Mental Health Act 1983 or the Mental Health (Scotland) Act 1984 (e.g. in a secure hospital or mental nursing home); or

☐ as a result of a court martial (except for open arrest or arrest of 48 hours or less).

3.36 The exemption does not apply in the case of detention resulting solely from non-payment of a fine or a community charge. It does not apply for a prisoner released on licence or parole, but does apply during any period of temporary discharge or temporary release on compassionate grounds.

3.37 The practice note (PN No. 19, paras. 3.4–9) suggests sample checks should be made verifying the validity of requests for exemption by or on behalf of prisoners (rather than requiring this in every case), and provides a form for use in cases where the registration officer wishes to confirm details with the prison service, along with a list of prison addresses.

MEMBERS OF RELIGIOUS COMMUNITIES

EW Act sch 1
para 7
S Act sch 1A
para 7

3.38 This exemption applies to anyone who is a member of a religious community who has no income or capital of his or her own – though an occupational pension from a former employment does not count. The community must have as its main occupation prayer, contemplation, relief of suffering, education or a combination of these; and the person must be dependent on the community for material needs.

3.39 The practice note (PN No. 19, paras. 10.1–3) advises that 'the test is intended to be strict and, with one or two exceptions, to include only those who do not have the means to pay the community charge'. Such persons are generally also excluded from receiving income support, housing benefit, etc, under social security rules. However, the words 'income' and 'capital' in the condition for exemption are not defined at all so that, e.g., the social security rules on resources do not necessarily apply.

VISITING ARMED FORCES, DIPLOMATS, ETC

EW Act sch 1
paras 2,3
S Act sch 1A
paras 2,3

3.40 This exemption applies (partly by Acts of Parliament, partly by international conventions) for:

☐ overseas diplomats of senior rank;
☐ military and civilian members of visiting forces (e.g. US forces);
☐ military and civilian members of certain international headquarters and international organisations; and
☐ in certain cases, the dependants of the above, e.g. a husband, wife or other person wholly or mainly maintained by them or in their custody, care or charge. Dependants are never exempt if they are themselves UK citizens or ordinarily resident in the UK, and there are various other rules.

3.41 The practice note, *Foreign Diplomats and Visiting Forces*, (PN No. 18) lists exactly who is exempt, and gives further advice on such questions as exactly when dependants are exempt, and what evidence may be obtained. Diplomats and members of certain international non-defence organisations are also exempt from standard and collective charges. Visiting forces and members of international headquarters and international defence organisations are not.

CROWN LAND

EW Act sch 1
para 11
S Act sch 1A
para 11

3.42 Most residents in Crown property are subject to the personal community charge. However certain Crown buildings are designated by the Secretary of State as exempt because most or all of the individuals who reside there:

☐ do so only for short periods (e.g. barracks where UK forces stay on training courses); or

☐ should not appear on the community charge register in the interests of national security;

3.43 The Ministry of Defence notifies registration officers of all such exemptions (PN No. 17, paras. 8.1–2). In Scotland, such premises are also not subject to a collective community charge (so no contributions are payable). In England and Wales, the Secretary of State intends to make a similar provision.

PEOPLE WHO PAY COLLECTIVE COMMUNITY CHARGE CONTRIBUTIONS

EW Act sch 1
para 12
S Act sch 1A
para 12

3.44 In Scotland, people who have to pay collective community charge contributions (Chapter 6) never have to pay a personal community charge as well. In England and Wales, this is true if their sole or main residence is at the address where they pay contributions. It is not true if their sole or main residence is elsewhere. This is illustrated in the following example.

Example

A man has a flat where he normally lives. He goes to look for work in another area and stays in a hostel where the landlord collects contributions. He only stays there for a couple of weeks, and it is decided that his sole or main residence is still at his flat.

If the hostel is in Scotland, he only has to pay a personal charge to the authority where his flat is.

If the hostel is in England or Wales, he has to pay a personal charge to the authority where his flat is and pay contributions in the hostel. (This would be true even if the hostel and the flat were in the same authority area.)

CHAPTER 4

The standard community charge

4.1 This chapter describes the standard community charge, which may have to be paid on domestic property which is no-one's home. It covers:

☐ who has to pay;
☐ what counts as domestic property;
☐ the amount of the charge; and
☐ multipliers and exemptions.

Who has to pay?

EW Act ss 3,4
S Act s 10

4.2 A standard community charge is due on each domestic property in England, Wales and Scotland which is no-one's sole or main residence. If a property is divided into self-contained parts, it applies to each part of the property which is domestic and which is no-one's sole or main residence. 'Sole or main residence' has the same meaning as in the case of the personal community charge (paras 2.23 onwards). The most common examples of property where a standard charge is due are second homes, holiday homes, and empty houses and flats owned by landlords. However, a number of kinds of property are exempt. In Scotland, people who have to pay a standard charge usually also have to pay the standard community water charge (para. 1.18).

EW Act ss 3,4
S Act s 10

4.3 The standard charge is due from the owner of the property or, in certain cases (para. 4.4), from a tenant. It applies whether the owner (or tenant) is an individual or a company or other organisation. For individuals, there is no lower age limit, nor are there any reductions in standard charges paid by students. Rules on 'joint and several liability' mean that if the owner (or tenant) of the property does not pay the charge, it may in some circumstances be collected from his or her partner (in the case of couples) or the manager of the property or a co-owner (paras 10.60 onwards).

EW Act ss 3,4
S Act s 10

4.4 The standard charge is only due from a tenant (including a sub-tenant) if the property is not the tenant's home. In England and Wales, this only applies for tenancies and licences granted for at least 6 months, and only if they confer exclusive possession. In Scotland, it only applies for tenancies granted for at least 12 months; other rules apply for tenancies of less than 12 months and all licences (para. 4.5).

Examples

STANDARD COMMUNITY CHARGE

A family own 2 homes, a main home in London (where they spend most of their time) and a holiday home in the New Forest (which they visit from time to time). Their holiday home is not used by anyone else.

They pay a standard community charge to the council in the New Forest where their holiday home is, because their holiday home is no-one's sole or main residence. This is in addition to the personal community charges they pay to the council in London where their main home is.

A couple own 2 homes, one where they live, the other where a relative lives.

No standard community charge is due, since each home is someone's sole or main residence.

A landlord owns a property which contains 4 self-contained flats. Flat A is the landlord's home. Flat B is let out to a family whose home it is. Flat C is on a 2-year lease to a tenant who uses it as a holiday home. Flat D has been empty for a long time.

No standard charge is due on Flats A or B, because each is someone's sole or main residence. A standard community charge is due on each of Flats C and D, because neither is anyone's sole or main residence. The tenant pays the standard charge on Flat C. The landlord pays the standard charge on Flat D.

STANDARD COMMUNITY CHARGE CONTRIBUTIONS

S Act s 10

4.5 In Scotland only, someone who is liable to pay a standard community charge may recover it from a tenant or licensee of the property. The amount recoverable is known as a 'standard community charge contribution'. This does not apply in the case of tenants and sub-tenants with a letting of at least 12 months, since they (and not the owner) are liable to pay the standard charge direct to the authority (para. 4.4). It does apply to tenants with a letting of less than 12 months, and all licensees. People who have to pay these standard contributions usually also have to pay standard community water charge contributions (para. 1.18).

4.6 The amount is calculated on a daily basis for the days when the letting exists, and limited to the amount due to the authority from the chargepayer for that period. Liability for a standard contribution is in addition to any liability to pay rent, and is not subject to any rule whatsoever relating to rent control. Rules on joint and several liability apply where there is more than one person liable to pay a standard contribution (paras 10.60 onwards). In England and Wales standard contributions do not exist.

Domestic vs. non-domestic

EW Act s 4
part III
S Act s 10
part I

4.7 Property is either domestic or non-domestic. A building can have one part which is domestic and one part which is non-domestic. The word 'property' in this chapter includes part of a building. Non-domestic property is subject to rates (unless charitable relief is granted): it is never subject to a standard community charge. Domestic property is not subject to rates and can be subject to a standard community charge. Usually, it is clear whether a property is domestic: any property used wholly for living accommodation is domestic. Some less straightforward cases are dealt with below. Further advice is given in the practice note, *The Standard Community Charge* (PN No. 13, paras. 2.7–9).

4.8 In England and Wales the decision about whether property is domestic for the purposes of a standard community charge is made by the community charge registration officer and is subject to appeal under the ordinary community charge appeal system (Chapter 12). In Scotland, this decision is made by the authority under its non-domestic rating duties, and it may therefore be necessary to conduct an appeal within the non-domestic rating appeals system (though the two systems are similar). If property is not currently in use, its status is decided in England and Wales by considering what appears to be its next use; in Scotland by considering its last use.

HOLIDAY ACCOMMODATION

4.9 Any property available for short-term letting for at least 140 days (20 weeks) in the year is classed as non-domestic. It is therefore subject to rates, and cannot attract a standard community charge. The property only has to be 'available' for such letting, not necessarily let. It is up to registration officers to interpret this, and what counts as 'short term' – their decisions may be appealed against (Chapter 13).

HOTELS AND OTHER ESTABLISHMENTS

EW Act s 10
S Act part I
S SI 1989
No.241

4.10 Hotels are non-domestic property, to the extent that they are used in the course of business, and the residents do not have their sole or main residence there. They are not therefore subject to standard community charges. However, staff accommodation is domestic property and may therefore be subject to a standard community charge. This can also apply to residential accommodation in boarding and lodging houses, public houses, educational establishments, fire stations, lighthouses, holiday camps, camping sites, etc.

WOMEN'S REFUGES

S Act s 2
S SI 1989
No.1477

4.11 In Scotland, women's refuges are classed as non-domestic property, and cannot therefore be subject to a standard community charge. In England and Wales, there is no such specific rule, so women's refuges could in theory attract a standard community charge.

COMMUNAL AREAS, OUTHOUSES, ETC

EW Act part III
S Act s 10
part I
S SI 1988
No.1477

4.12 Communal areas (e.g. in care homes, nursing homes, hostels, sheltered housing, etc), outhouses and private storage premises are not subject to a standard community charge, so long as they are part of a domestic property, and are not intended as residential accommodation. Sheds and huts are not subject to a standard community charge so long as they are not intended as residential accommodation.

MOBILE HOMES, CARAVANS AND HOUSEBOATS

EW Act ss 3,4,
31
S Act s 2
S SI 1989
No.241

4.13 Mobile homes in local authority licensed, or local authority owned, mobile home parks can be subject to a standard community charge. So can caravans on certain other kinds of licensed site in Scotland. If a standard charge is due under this heading, it is always due from the owner (and para. 4.3 does not apply). All other caravans (such as a touring caravan or a caravan kept in somebody's garden or yard), and all houseboats, cannot be subject to a standard charge.

ACCOMMODATION STRADDLING BOUNDARIES

EW Act ss 4,
14,31
EW regs 53,54
57

4.14 If a property straddles the boundary of 2 or more areas, it is treated as being in the area where the greater or greatest part is (as described in para. 2.39). In the case of a building with self-contained parts, all the parts are then treated as being in that area.

The amount of the charge

ANNUAL AMOUNT

EW Act s 14
S Act s 10

4.15 If the chargepayer is liable for a standard charge for the whole financial year, the whole annual amount is due. This is calculated by multiplying the authority's personal community charge for the year (or the personal charge for the appropriate area within the authority) by a figure known as the standard community charge multiplier (described in para. 4.19) – or 'multiplier' for short:

☐   Personal community charge × multiplier = standard community charge.

Example

STANDARD COMMUNITY CHARGE CALCULATION

A woman has a second home which is not exempt from the standard community charge. The local council has a personal community charge of £300, and decides that the multiplier for her property is 2.

Her standard community charge for the year is therefore £300 × 2 = £600.

PART-YEAR AMOUNT

EW Act ss 7,14
S Act s 11A

4.16 If the chargepayer is liable for a standard community charge for only a part of a financial year, the amount is worked out on a daily basis for the appropriate period:

☐   divide the annual amount by the number of days of the financial year (365 or 366); and

☐ multiply the result by the number of days in the financial year on which the chargepayer is liable for the charge. The financial year runs from 1 April to 31 March. If the chargepayer is liable for the charge for 2 (or more) properties or 2 (or more) unconnected periods for the same property, the charge for each period and each property is calculated separately.

EW Act ss 7,8,
14

4.17 When a standard charge is calculated on a daily basis:

S Act s 11A

☐ a day on which the chargepayer starts to be liable for the charge is counted;

☐ a day on which the chargepayer ceases to be liable for the charge is not counted;

☐ a day on which the chargepayer both starts and ceases to be liable for the charge is not counted;

☐ on a day when the property changes from one class to the other (so that the multiplier changes), it is counted as belonging to the class to which it belongs latest in that day.

OTHER FACTORS

4.18 Future changes in the chargepayer's circumstances are not taken into account, so bills sent out at the beginning of the year are always for the whole annual amount, and bills sent out at the beginning of any part-year period are always for the remainder of the financial year. In each case, adjustments are made only when relevant changes actually occur (Chapter 10). In almost all cases, standard charges may be paid by instalments, in which case additional rules apply (Chapter 10).

Multipliers and exemptions

EW Act s 40
S Act s 10

4.19 Properties subject to the standard community charge are divided into various classes, and each authority sets a standard community charge multiplier for each class of property (so the multiplier for a particular class of property may vary from one authority to another). Multipliers must be set in advance of a financial year, and for the whole of that year: they cannot be varied during the financial year.

EW Act s 40
S Act s 10

4.20 Authorities are only permitted to set multipliers of 0, $1/_2$, 1, $1^1/_2$ or 2 (other fractions are not allowed). Setting a multiplier of 0 has the effect that the property is exempt: no standard community charge is due. (The rules were different in Scotland during the 1989/90 financial year: para. 4.24.)

CLASSES OF PROPERTY LAID DOWN IN LAW

EW Act s 40
EW reg 62
S Act s 10

4.21 A number of classes are laid down in law. These are summarised in the following table (4.1). In some of these cases, there are further limitations on the amount of the multiplier:

- [ ] for some classes, the authority must set a multiplier of 0 (or exempt them);
- [ ] for other classes, the authority must set a multiplier of either 0, $^1/_2$ or 1;
- [ ] for all other classes, there are no limitations: the authority may set a multiplier of 0, $^1/_2$, 1, $1^1/_2$ or 2.

Table 4.1

**STANDARD COMMUNITY CHARGE:
CLASSES OF PROPERTY LAID DOWN IN LAW**

In most cases there are further conditions described in the text

Properties where no standard charge is due

- [ ] Any unfurnished property, for the first 3 months
- [ ] Property where the former occupier is now in a hospital, residential care home, nursing home or hostel
- [ ] Property left vacant by a carer
- [ ] Unfurnished property undergoing repair, alteration, etc
- [ ] Property which is empty following a death
- [ ] Property normally used by a minister of religion
- [ ] Property where the former occupier is in prison or is a full-time student in advanced education (Scotland only)
- [ ] Certain unfurnished agricultural dwellings (Scotland only)
- [ ] Housing association temporary accommodation for the elderly or disabled (Scotland only)
- [ ] Property whose occupation is prohibited by law

Properties where the multiplier can only be 0, $^1/_2$ or 1

- [ ] Mobile homes (England and Wales only)
- [ ] Property where year-round occupation is prohibited (England and Wales only)

CLASSES OF PROPERTY CREATED BY AUTHORITIES

EW Act s 40
S Act s 10
S SI 1989
No.2437

4.22 Authorities may also create further classes (or sub-classes), amend them and revoke them; but only in advance of a financial year, and for the whole of that year. In England and Wales, when an authority does create a new class, it must publish the details in at least one newspaper circulating in its area. In Scotland, only regional and islands councils may create further classes, but the multipliers for these classes may vary on a district by district basis (regardless of whether the district authority or the regional authority collects the community charge).

EW Act s 40
S Act s 10
S SI 1989
No.2437

4.23 However, authorities cannot create a new class that would have the effect of increasing the multiplier for any property within it above any limitation laid down in law. In England and Wales, authorities may specify further classes only by reference to:

- ☐ the use to which properties are intended to be put;
- ☐ whether properties are occupied;
- ☐ the period for which properties have been unoccupied;
- ☐ the circumstances, other than financial, of persons subject to a standard charge;
- ☐ the capacity in which they are subject to a standard charge; and
- ☐ whether properties already fall within a class laid down in law.

In Scotland, authorities may specify further classes of property only by reference to:

- ☐ the period during which they have not been the sole or main residence of any person;
- ☐ the past, present or intended use of the property; and
- ☐ the circumstances, other than financial, of persons subject to a standard charge.

RULES IN SCOTLAND

4.24 For the 1989-90 financial year, the system of multipliers in Scotland was different. All the properties within a particular authority area had the same multiplier (unless they were exempt), which could be any amount between 1 and 2 including fractions, but not less than 1. The exempt groups of property were also different.

UNFURNISHED PROPERTY IN GENERAL

EW reg 62
S Act s 10

4.25 No standard charge is due on any property for the first 3 months that it is unoccupied and substantially unfurnished. A property counts as unoccupied if no-one lives there at all. A property is not treated as unoccupied on the day when an occupier begins or ceases to occupy it. There is no definition of when a property is 'substantially unfurnished'. Interpretation is left to the discretion of individual registration officers and could form the basis for an appeal.

S Act s 10

4.26 In Scotland, there is a specific rule that a person who wishes to take advantage of this exemption must notify the registration officer that the property is unoccupied and unfurnished. The exemption cannot be backdated more than one month before this occurs. In England and Wales, although it is usually necessary to request exemption, this is not required in law; and the ordinary 2-year limit on backdating applies (paras 8.14 onwards). Under both sets of rules, the exemption still lasts for 3 months from the first day when it first applies.

EW reg 62
S Act s 10

4.27 The exemption is laid down in law for the first 3 months. After that authorities may extend the time limit by specifying a further class of exempt property (para. 4.43). In Scotland, the 3 months' exemption can only apply once during any period when a standard charge applies (or would apply apart from the exemption), and there are no 'linking rules'.

EW reg 62

4.28 In England and Wales, 'linking rules' apply as follows for properties which have been unoccupied:

☐ if anyone occupies the property for 6 weeks or more, a fresh period of exemption begins (whether the previous period of exemption has expired or not);

☐ if anyone occupies the property for less than 6 weeks, no fresh period of exemption begins (though any unused part of a previous period of exemption continues).

Examples

ENGLAND AND WALES: LINKING RULE

A property is vacated permanently on 21 September. In this and the following example, the property is unfurnished when vacated.

It is exempt from a standard charge from 21 September to 20 December inclusive.

A property is vacated on 21 September, and then re-occupied from 1 October to 31 December inclusive.

It is exempt from a standard charge from 21 to 30 September inclusive. The occupation from 1 October to 31 December is more than 6 weeks. From 31 December onwards a new 3 months' exemption applies, which lasts until 30 March.

A property is vacated on 21 September, and then re-occupied from 1 to 11 October inclusive.

It is exempt from a standard charge from 21 to 30 September inclusive. The occupation from 1 to 10 October is for 10 days. So the property is exempt again from 11 October to 30 December inclusive (10 days later than in the first example above).

A property is vacated on 21 September, and then re-occupied from the following 26 February to 19 April inclusive.

It is exempt from a standard charge from 21 September to 20 December inclusive. The occupation from 26 February to 19 April is more than 6 weeks. From 19 April onwards a new 3 months' exemption applies, which lasts until 18 March.

WHEN A FORMER OCCUPIER IS NOW IN HOSPITAL, ETC OR IS NOW A CARER

EW reg 62
S SI 1989
No.2437

4.29 No standard charge is due on any property if the person who would otherwise have to pay it previously occupied it as his or her sole or main residence and:

- [ ] is exempt from a personal community charge because of being solely or mainly resident in a hospital, residential care home, nursing home, or hostel (paras 3.15–25), or detained under the Mental Health Acts in a hospital or a nursing home (para. 3.35); and
- [ ] is solely or main resident in, and receiving personal care in, similar accommodation (e.g. a private hospital – where exemption from a personal community charge does not apply); or
- [ ] is solely or mainly resident in any accommodation (including, for example, a private residence) in order to *provide* care.

EW reg 62
S SI 1989
No.2437

4.30 It is not necessary for the property to be unfurnished. However, in England and Wales, it must be unoccupied – i.e. no-one must live there at all. It is not counted as unoccupied on the day when an occupier begins or ceases to occupy it. Difficulties in establishing when someone begins to be solely or mainly resident in a hospital, home or hostel, and possible solutions, are discussed in paras 3.16 onwards.

EW reg 62
S SI 1989
No.2437

4.31 In Scotland the exemption begins when the last sole or main resident leaves the property, and is laid down in law as lasting indefinitely. In England and Wales, the exemption begins when the last occupier (of any kind) leaves the property, and is laid down in law as lasting for 12 months. English and Welsh authorities who wish to extend this period (and avoid the other restrictions discussed below) can specify a further class of exempt property (para. 4.43), and should be encouraged to do so.

EW regs 59,62
S SI 1989
No.2437

4.32 Once the exemption has begun to apply, the position becomes more complicated. The issues are summarised in Table 4.2 and some are illustrated in the following examples, but it should be noted that less harsh interpretations may be argued for in some of the English and Welsh cases described there. Indeed, it appears in some of these that the relevant statutory instrument must have been drafted badly.

Table 4.2

WHERE THE FORMER OCCUPIER IS IN HOSPITAL, ETC: FURTHER ISSUES

Issue	England and Wales	Scotland
Another sole or main resident (a) moves into the property; (b) moves out again. (The property does not change hands.)	(a) Liability for a standard charge ends. (b) A fresh 12 months' period of exemption begins.	(a) Liability for a standard charge ends. (b) Exemption continues indefinitely (regardless of how long that person was there).
Another occupier (not a sole or main resident) (a) moves into the property; (b) moves out again.	(a) Exemption ceases. (b) A fresh 12 months' period of exemption begins.	(a) and (b) Exemption continues indefinitely.
The exempt person moves to a new hospital, etc.	The same 12 months' period of exemption continues.	Exemption continues indefinitely.
The property is owned/ rented by a couple (a) in joint names; (b) in one name only.	(a) Same as for joint owners/tenants (below). (b) Exemption only applies if the one in whose name it is satisfies the conditions (para. 4.29).[1]	(a) and (b) Same as for joint owners/tenants (below).
The property is jointly owned/rented other than by a couple.	Exemption only applies if the last such sole or main resident satisfies the conditions para. 4.29).[1]	Exemption applies as long as at least one of them fulfils the conditions (para. 4.29).

1. On these somewhat harsh interpretations see para. 4.32.

Examples

A woman lives in her house with a lodger. For both of them, it is their sole residence. On 26 February 1991 the woman moves permanently into a nursing home where she is exempt from a personal community charge. The lodger remains until 19 April 1992. The house is then unoccupied. The authority for the area has not created any classes of exemption beyond those laid down in law.

From 19 April 1992, the woman is exempt from a standard charge. In Scotland this lasts indefinitely. In England and Wales it lasts until 18 April 1993, after which the woman is no longer exempt.

On 26 July 1994, a relative of the above woman goes to stay in the house, and stays there until 21 September 1994. For that period, it is the relative's sole residence.

From 26 July to 20 September 1994, the relative has to pay a personal charge, and so no standard charge arises.

From 21 September 1994, the woman is once again exempt from a standard charge. In Scotland this again lasts indefinitely. In England and Wales it lasts until 20 September 1995, after which the woman is no longer exempt.

PROPERTIES UNDERGOING REPAIR, ALTERATION, ETC

EW reg 62
S SI 1989
No.2437

4.33 No standard community charge is due on any property which is substantially unfurnished and unoccupied (i.e. no-one lives there at all) and is undergoing repair, alteration, etc. The exact details as laid down in law are slightly different between England and Wales, and Scotland.

EW reg 62

4.34 In England and Wales, the exemption only applies if the property:

☐ requires structural repair works to render it habitable (though work need not have started);
☐ is being built and is not substantially completed; or

☐ is in the course or structural alteration which has not been substantially completed (and work must have started);

– and in each case the exemption continues for 6 months after the work is substantially completed (so long as the property remains unoccupied).

S SI 1989
No.2437

4.35 In Scotland, the exemption only applies if the the property:

☐ is incapable of being lived in because it is being repaired, improved, or reconstructed (and work must have started);

– and the only time limit is that the exemption ceases as soon as the work is abandoned or completed. There is no 6 months' extension, though authorities may specify a new class of exemption allowing for this.

4.36 The questions of what counts as 'substantially unfurnished', 'structural repair works', 'structural alteration', 'repaired', 'improved', 'reconstructed', 'habitable', 'incapable of being lived in' and 'substantially completed' are all left to the discretion of the registration officer, and can be subject to appeal.

PROPERTIES EMPTY FOLLOWING A DEATH

EW reg 62
S SI 1989
No.2437

4.37 In England and Wales, property is exempt from a standard community charge if it is unoccupied (i.e. no-one must live there at all) and the person concerned is the personal representative of someone who has died. It applies until the person receives grant of probate or letters of administration (i.e. acquires the power to dispose of the property), and for 3 months after that. In Scotland, no standard charge is due for 6 months following the death of someone who was exempt from a personal charge because of being in hospital, etc. (paras 3.15–25). No general exemption applies as in England and Wales. However, there is nothing to stop any authority specifying a new class allowing for a wider range of exemptions (para. 4.23).

PROPERTY USED BY MINISTERS OF RELIGION

EW reg 62
S SI 1989
No.2437

4.38 No standard charge is due on any unoccupied property which is being kept available for a minister of religion for the performance of his or her duties. 'Minister of religion' is not defined, and there is no time limit.

PROPERTY WHERE THE FORMER OCCUPIER IS IN PRISON OR IS A REGISTERED STUDENT

S SI 1989
No.2437

4.39 In Scotland only, no standard charge is due if the former occupier is now in prison or any other form of detention (paras 3.35–36) and is thereby exempt from a personal charge; nor if the former occupier is a student in full-time advanced education and thereby qualifies to pay only 20 per cent of the personal charge (paras 2.10 onwards).

AGRICULTURAL DWELLINGS

S SI 1989
No.2437

4.40 In Scotland only, no standard charge is due on any unoccupied, unfurnished property previously used in conjunction with, and located on:

☐   agricultural or pastoral land; or
☐   woodlands, market gardens, orchards or allotments; or
☐   land exceeding $^1/_{10}$ hectare used for poultry farming.

HOUSING ASSOCIATION TEMPORARY ACCOMMODATION FOR THE ELDERLY OR DISABLED

S SI 1989
No.2437

4.41 In Scotland only, no standard charge is due on property held by a registered housing association, which has been specially designed or adapted for people of pensionable age or disabled people under the Housing (Scotland) Act 1987, and which is intended for their use prior to finding them permanent equivalent accommodation.

PROPERTIES WHERE OCCUPATION IS PROHIBITED BY LAW

EW reg 62
S SI 1989
No.2437

4.42 No standard charge is due on any property which is unoccupied because it is subject to a closing order, demolition order or compulsory purchase order.

MOBILE HOMES

EW reg 62

4.43 In England and Wales only, the standard community charge for a mobile home can only be 0, $^1/_2$ or 1 (at the discretion of the authority), but no greater. This rule is not laid down in law in Scotland, though authorities may specify a new class of exemption making a similar provision.

PROPERTIES WHERE YEAR-ROUND OCCUPATION IS PROHIBITED

EW reg 62

4.44 In England and Wales only, the standard community charge for a property can only be 0, $^1/_2$ or 1 (at the discretion of the authority), but no greater, if planning permission for the property prevents occupation throughout the year. For example, this may apply for certain types of holiday accommodation. This rule is not laid down in law in Scotland, though authorities may specify a new class of exemption making a similar provision.

CROWN PROPERTY

EW Act s 21
S Act s 30

4.45 The Crown (e.g. government departments, etc) does not have to pay a standard community charge. In England and Wales this applies except when the property is maintained by a local authority for the purposes of administration of justice, police purposes or other Crown purposes. This exemption does not prevent someone else who holds an interest in Crown property (e.g. a tenant) from having to pay a standard charge.

PROPERTY SUBJECT TO A COLLECTIVE COMMUNITY CHARGE

EW Act s 3

4.46 In England and Wales only, property subject to a collective community charge is specifically excluded from liability for a standard charge.

OTHER PROPERTY

4.47 For all properties other than those described above, authorities may set a standard community charge multiplier of 0, $^1/_2$, 1, $1^1/_2$ or 2, and may create further classes which have different multipliers within that range, including creating further exempt classes (paras 4.22–23).

CHAPTER 5

The collective community charge

5.1 This chapter considers:

☐ which types of property are subject to the collective charge;
☐ who must pay the charge;
☐ the amount of charge payable by the landlord; and
☐ the records which must be kept by landlords.

5.2 The collective charge is made in respect of property where there is a high turnover of very mobile people from whom it would be difficult for the authority to collect personal charge payments, e.g. short-stay hostels, lodging houses and some houses in multiple occupation (HMOs). In Scotland where the necessary conditions are met (para. 1.18) a collective water charge is also payable. Liability to pay these charges is usually placed upon the owner or lessee of the dwelling. In this and the following chapters such chargeable persons are referred to as 'landlords'. The people who stay in these properties are called 'residents'. Most residents are required to pay amounts, known as contributions (Chapter 6), to the landlord. The landlord must supply receipts for such payments (para. 6.26). This chapter should be read in conjunction with Chapter 6. The authority's demand notice and the returns/payments which must be made by English and Welsh landlords are examined in Chapter 10.

5.3 *The Collective Community Charge* (PN No. 14, para. 2.1) emphasises that the collective charge is intended to be the exception rather than the rule: 'Wherever it is possible to operate through the normal arrangements of the personal charge this is the approach which should be adopted'. The same sentiment was expressed by Ministers in relation to Scotland during the Scottish Bill's committee stages.

Property subject to the charge

EW Act s 5   **5.4** Property is subject to the collective charge on any day it is desig-
S Act s 11   nated as such by the registration officer. In Scotland the Secretary of
State may also prescribe that certain classes of premises are subject
to the charge.

DESIGNATED BUILDINGS

EW Act s 5   **5.5** The registration officer may designate all or part of a building if:
S Act s 11

☐   it is in the authority's area;
☐   in the registration officer's opinion (part of) the building is used
wholly or mainly as the sole or main residence of individuals
most of whom reside there for a short period and are not registered students undertaking a full-time course of education (para.
2.10);
☐   in England and Wales the registration officer is of the opinion
that it would probably be difficult to maintain the register in
respect of, and collect personal charge payments from, individuals occupying the premises; and
☐   the building is not exempt.

5.6 PN No. 14 (para. 2.2) recommends that registration officers
take a cautious approach and 'refrain from designating buildings
unless they are absolutely certain that individual registration is not
feasible'.

5.7 The condition that (part of) the designated building be the sole
or main residence of individuals excludes the owners of non-domestic
properties, e.g. hotels and guest houses, from liability for the collective charge for those buildings. The exclusion of premises subject to
non-domestic rates is explicit in the Scottish Act.

5.8 The regulations do not define what is meant by a short period.
This is for the registration officer to decide. For designation to occur
it is not necessary for all residents to be short-term, only that most
stay for short periods. If most of the residents are full-time students
the building is not designated. Part of a building may be designated.
This could occur, e.g., where resident staff permanently occupy
another part of the building. In such circumstances they would be
liable for the personal charge (Chapter 2).

EW Act s 5   **5.9** If the building crosses a boundary between authorities it is treated as situated in the authority in which the greatest part of the building is situated (para. 2.39).

5.10 In Scotland there in no requirement that the registration officer should also consider that it would probably be difficult to maintain the register in respect of, and collect personal charge payments from, individuals occupying those premises. However, the discretionary nature of designation means that designation does not normally happen unless this is the case.

S Act s 11
S SI 1989
No.631
S SI 1989
No.1476
S SI 1989
No.1477

5.11 At the time of writing there are no class of premises in Scotland that are prescribed by the Secretary of State for the purpose of the collective community charge. Women's refuges were originally prescribed under this rule, but from 4 September 1989 they have been treated as liable for non-domestic rates and therefore not liable for the collective charge.

EXEMPT BUILDINGS

EW reg 58   **5.12** In England and Wales exempt buildings are hostels (such as those provided by the Salvation Army), night shelters or other buildings, which provide residential accommodation predominantly:

☐ for people who have no fixed abode and no settled way of life;
☐ in other than separate and self-contained premises;
☐ under licences (rather than tenancies).

Such exempt dwellings are free from the collective charge and their residents free from the personal charge (para. 3.27).

S Act s 11   **5.13** In Scotland the Secretary of State also has the power to exempt certain types of premises from the collective charge. It is intended that this power be used in the same way as it has been in England and Wales. To date this has not happened.

START AND END OF DESIGNATION

EW Act s 5
S Act s 11

5.14 In England and Wales designation only takes effect 7 days after it is made. Throughout Great Britain it may be revoked at any time if the necessary conditions no longer exist.

Who must pay the collective charge?

EW Act s 5   **5.15** The policy aim for England, Wales and Scotland is that the person with the closest contact and responsibility for the property, and therefore the greatest likelihood of collecting contributions from residents, should be the one responsible for paying the collective charge. In England and Wales the person who must pay the collective charge – the landlord – is the person who:

☐ has a 'qualifying interest' in the dwelling;

☐ is entered in the register as liable for the charge; or

☐ someone who is jointly and severally liable with that person (para. 10.60).

5.16 The owner of the freehold of the whole dwelling is the person who has the qualifying interest unless there is a leaseholder of the whole dwelling. In the latter circumstance that person has the qualifying interest. Where there is more than one leaseholder, liability falls on the holder of the inferior lease. For example, where the original lessee grants a lease of the same property to someone for a shorter term the latter person is liable for the collective charge.

S Act s 11   **5.17** In Scotland liability follows the same pattern. The person liable for the charge is the owner, or , if the premises are let for 12 months or more, the tenant and if they are sub-let for 12 months or more the sub-tenant.

5.18 A registered student in full-time advanced education (para. 2.10), who is also a landlord and liable for the collective charge, must pay the full collective charge.

EW Act s 5   **5.19** The landlord's liability begins and ends when his or her legal
S Act s 11   interest in the property begins and ends. In England and Wales management agents and throughout Great Britain co-owners are jointly and severally liable with the landlord for the collective charge (para. 10.60).

The amount of collective charge payable

5.20 The manner in which the amount of collective charge payable is worked out is significantly different in Scotland from England and

Wales. In either case, the landlord is liable to pay the collective charge whether or not contributions have been paid by the residents. The landlord may take steps to recover unpaid contributions through the courts but the authority has no direct interest in such preceedings.

ENGLAND AND WALES

EW Act sch 2 paras 2,3

5.21 Normally within 14 days of the end of each calender month (a 'return period') an English or Welsh landlord must make a return to the authority (paras 10.49–51) that states the contributions payable within the return period and includes payment for that period.

EW Act ss 5,15

5.22 The collective charge payable by the landlord for the return period is:

☐ the sum of the contributions payable by the residents during that period;

☐ minus 5 per cent – which the landlord keeps to meet administrative expenses.

5.23 The contributions payable by a resident are the daily equivalent of the annual personal charge. This is worked out as follows:

☐ personal charge;

☐ divided by the number of days in the year (365 or 366);

☐ multiplied by the number of days he or she is resident in the designated dwelling during the return period.

Example

The landlord has 3 qualifying residents during May 1990. The 3 spend the following days in the property during that month – 2, 5, and 10. Thus the total number of resident days in the return period (May) amounts to 17 – i.e, 2+5+10.

The daily charge is the annual personal charge (£650) divided by the number of days in the year (365) i.e. £1.78.

The sum of the contributions payable by the residents is £30.26, i.e., £1.78 × 17.

The collective charge payable by the landlord for that return period is £28.75 i.e. 95% × £30.26.

SCOTLAND

S Act s 11   **5.24** The annual collective charge payable by the Scottish landlord is:

☐ the island's or the region's and district's personal charge;
☐ multiplied by the collective charge multiplier;
☐ minus 5 per cent which the landlord keeps to meet administrative expenses.

AMOUNT FOR A PERIOD

5.25 Where the period for which the charge is payable is only part of a financial year, e.g., where a hostel has opened part way through the year or the community charge multiplier has been amended following a change in the maximum number of persons who can be accommodated, the amount payable for the period is:

☐ the annual charge;
☐ divided by the number of days in the year;
☐ multiplied by the number of days in the period for which the new or amended charge is payable.

5.26 The collective water charge is calculated in the same manner using the personal water charge in place of the personal community charge in the above formula.

THE COLLECTIVE CHARGE MULTIPLIER

S Act s 11
S SI 1988
No.631

5.27 The collective charge multiplier is a key element in working out the Scottish landlord's collective charge. It is an amount determined by the registration officer. In setting the multiplier the registration officer must have regard to:

☐ the numbers of persons solely or mainly resident in the premises who would otherwise be liable to pay the personal charge;
☐ the maximum number of people for whom the premises are capable of providing residential accommodation;
☐ the number of people who at any time during the 3 months immediately prior to the determination of a multiplier were solely or mainly resident in the premises; and
☐ where a multiplier has previously been determined – the extent to which the number of persons solely or mainly resident in the premises during the period the current multiplier has been in force is greater, or less than, the number of persons to which the registration officer had regard when the current multiplier was determined.

In determining the multiplier the registration officer takes no account of registered students.

AMENDMENTS TO THE MULTIPLIER

S Act ss 11,15

5.28 One of the main factors which is reflected in the multiplier is the number of residents solely or mainly resident in the premises who would otherwise be liable to the personal charge. This figure may change throughout the year. These changes are not completely reflected in amendments to the multiplier figure. They may only be made at intervals of at least 3 months. Furthermore, once such an amendment has taken place it must be assumed for the purpose of calculating the collective charge that the amended multiplier is not further amended for the remainder of the financial year.

5.29 It can be seen then that the multiplier does not always equal the actual number of people in the premises who are liable to pay contributions at any one time. In this respect the Scottish collective charge is particularly different from its English and Welsh equivalent.

S Act ss 15,16   **5.30** Alterations to the multiplier figure in the register entry may be made by the registration officer at any time to:

☐ correct a typographical or clerical error; or
☐ to give effect to the decision of a sheriff or higher judge on a registration appeal (Chapter 12).

THE LANDLORD'S DUTY TO REPORT CHANGES OF CIRCUMSTANCE

S Act s 18   **5.31** The Scottish landlord must notify the registration officer of any change in circumstance which would effect the register entry within one month. For example, a change in the number of bed spaces that would influence the multiplier item. Where such events are notified later than one month after they take place 10 per cent interest is payable by the landlord on the collective charge due between the end of that month and the day the amended entry is made to the register.

5.32 If the period between the date of the event and the date of the amendment being made to the register is greater than 3 months, and the landlord does not have a reasonable excuse for failing to notify the registration officer sooner, then a surcharge of 30 per cent of the total amount due or £50, which ever is the greater, becomes payable.

The landlord's records

EW Act Sch 2   **5.33** In England and Wales the landlord must keep records showing:

☐ the name of all individuals resident in the dwelling who must pay contributions;
☐ the periods during which they are resident;
☐ the contribution payable for each day by the individuals.

5.34 Only qualifying individuals (para. 6.6) are required to pay contributions; others are exempt. The landlord's records relate solely to qualifying individuals. The landlord must consider whether or not a resident is exempt (para. 6.7). Exempt cases should not arise frequently because the great majority of exempt individuals never stay in designated buildings. The one exception to this 'rule' are full-time students. They should be able to satisfy the landlord that they are exempt by producing student certificates (para. 2.16). Where the landlord is suspicious he or she may seek confirmation of the individual's student status from the registration officer.

5.35 The regulations do not prescribe a standard format for the records. PN No. 14 (para. 4.1) suggests that charging authorities may supply standard pro formas if they wish, though landlords do not have to use them.

EW regs
sch 2 para 1

5.36 The landlord must keep these records for at least one year after the end of the contribution period to which they relate.

PENALTIES FOR NOT COMPILING OR KEEPING RECORDS

EW Act sch 3
para 2

5.37 The registration officer may fine the English or Welsh landlord £50 if the landlord fails to compile or retain collective charge records. For each repeated breach of this duty the registration officer may impose a £200 penalty (para. 11.6).

EXAMINATION OF THE LANDLORD'S RECORDS

EW regs
sch 2 para 1

5.38 In England and Wales the registration officer and the authority have the right to examine the landlord's records. This may be done in one of 2 ways. The registration officer or the authority may make a written request:

☐   to inspect the landlord's records; or
☐   for a copy of the records.

EW Act sch 3
paras 1,2

5.39 The landlord must allow inspection within 5 days of the request having been made and supply a copy of the records within 21 days. If the landlord fails to meet these requirements, without reasonable excuse, the authority or registration officer that made the request may impose a £50 penalty (paras 11.4–6). For each repeated breach of the same duty without reasonable excuse a £200 penalty may be imposed. Falsification of records by a landlord with the objective of avoiding payment is a criminal offence under the Theft Act.

EW reg 12   **5.40** Where an English or Welsh registration officer or authority has copies of the landlord's records it must allow them to be inspected by any resident who is liable to pay contributions to that landlord (para. 9.24).

THE SCOTTISH LANDLORD'S RECORDS

S Act s 11   **5.41** In Scotland the landlord must maintain a record of:

☐ all individuals solely or mainly resident in the premises (including those exempt from paying contributions);
☐ the periods during which individuals are resident;
☐ the amount of contributions paid.

5.42 These records are an important source of information for the registration officer in setting the collective charge multiplier. They could also prove an important source of evidence in any appeal. Scottish residents have no right to inspect them.

CHAPTER 6

Collective community charge contributions

6.1 This chapter looks at the contributions which must be paid by certain residents to landlords liable for the collective charge. It considers:

- [ ] who must pay contributions;
- [ ] the notification they must be provided with;
- [ ] the time and amount of payment;
- [ ] other matters relating to contributions.

6.2 The resident's obligation is to the landlord. There is no formal relationship between the authority and the resident. If the resident fails to pay contributions the landlord may recover the outstanding amount through the courts. In Scotland where a collective water charge is payable residents who must pay contributions must also pay collective water charge contributions. The rules about the joint and several liability of partners (para. 10.61) do not apply to residents. Residents have little by way of appeal rights (para. 12.3). Community charge benefit (Chapter 7) is available to help low income residents pay contributions.

6.3 The rules relating to contributions are significantly different for Scotland than those for England and Wales.

Who must pay contributions?

EW Act s 9   **6.4** In England and Wales individuals need only pay contributions if:

- [ ] resident in a designated dwelling (para. 5.5);

☐   a qualifying individual (para. 6.6); and
☐   the landlord is shown in the register as subject to the authority's collective charge for that dwelling.

6.5 All qualifying individuals who are resident in a building must pay contributions whether or not the dwelling is their sole or main residence. Those who are solely or mainly resident pay contributions instead of the personal charge. Temporary residents have to pay contributions for each day they reside in the property as well as any personal charge they may be liable for. The position is different in Scotland (para. 6.9).

QUALIFYING INDIVIDUALS

EW Act s 11   **6.6** Individuals count as qualifying on any day that they are:

☐   aged 18 or over;
☐   not exempt;
☐   not registered students in a period during which they are undertaking a full-time course of advanced education.

6.7 Individuals who are exempt from the personal charge (Chapter 3) are exempt from making contributions, except the following for any day they reside in a building designated for the purpose of the collective charge:

☐   occupants of certain Crown buildings which have been designated by the Secretary of State (para. 3.42);
☐   people sleeping rough (of no fixed abode – anyone resident in a building at the end of the day is not entitled to this exemption);
☐   full-time students whose term-time address is in Northern Ireland or Scotland.
☐   people whose sole or main residence is in a property designated for the collective charge.

6.8 Full-time students who are resident in England and Wales for the purpose of undertaking their course are not qualifying individuals. They are not liable to pay contributions. Such students should be registered for the authority's personal charge.

6.9 In Scotland individuals must pay contributions to the landlord for each day they are:

☐ solely or mainly resident in premises subject to the collective charge; and

☐ would be liable for the personal charge if they were not in such premises.

6.10 Additionally in Scotland registered students are exempt from the payment of contributions but must pay 20 per cent of the personal charge if the premises are in the area of the authority in which they are resident during term-time for the purpose of undertaking their course. As registered students they are not liable for any community charge outside that area.

6.11 The requirement that the resident must solely or mainly reside in the premises differs significantly from the requirement in England and Wales and may be particularly difficult to determine, e.g., during a relationship breakdown.

6.12 Residents who think that they are exempt should make that fact known to the landlord. The landlord must decide whether or not to treat a resident as exempt. Exempt residents who experience difficulties with the landlord on this matter should seek the assistance of the registration officer or an advice agency (para. 3.6). In the case of students landlords may require sight of the certificate supplied by their educational establishments which certifies that they are in full-time education (para. 2.16). The landlord may also seek confirmation of the individual's student status from the registration officer.

START AND END OF RESIDENCE

EW Act s 11
S Act s 11

6.13 The resident is counted as residing in the dwelling from the day residence is taken up to the day before departure. Individuals who take up residence and depart the building on the same day are not counted as resident in the dwelling.

Notification to residents of contribution liability

EW SI 1989
No.438 sch 2
para 5

6.14 Residents in England and Wales must be notified by the landlord of their liability for contributions as soon as practicable after:

☐ a building is designated and the landlord is served with a demand notice; or

☐ the individual takes up residence.

6.15 The notification must inform residents that the building is designated. It must also supply them with information about the amount which is payable and the days on which it is due. As a matter of good practice the landlord should also supply each resident with a community charge benefit claim form. The landlord may obtain these from the authority. In practice the above should also happen in Scotland.

EW Act sch 3
para 2

6.16 If the English or Welsh landlord fails, without reasonable excuse, to provide residents with this information the registration officer may impose a £50 penalty.

6.17 Where the authority serves notice on the landlord that a new personal charge has been set which differs from that for the previous year the landlord must inform residents of the new amount which is payable.

S Act s 11

6.18 In Scotland a resident does not have to pay a contribution until the landlord has given him or her notification of the daily amount. No contributions are payable for any day before this notification is given.

Time of payment

EW Act sch 2
para 6

6.19 In England or Wales if the resident must make payments for the accommodation at intervals of a month or less, contributions must be paid on the same days as the accommodation payments are made. These days are called 'rent days'. The landlord decides whether the contributions paid on those days should be in advance or arrears (i.e. for the period after the rent day to the next rent day, or for the period on or before the rent day).

6.20 In England and Wales where no accommodation payments are made, or are not made at intervals of a month or less, contributions must be paid on 'payment days'. These are decided by the landlord. Intervals between payment days must not be greater than monthly. Again payments must be made in advance or arrears as decided by the landlord.

Amount of the contribution

EW Act ss 9,10   **6.21** The contribution payable by a resident in England or Wales is based on the authority's personal charge. For each day the resident is in the designated dwelling he or she is liable to pay the daily equivalent of the personal charge last set before the day began, rounded to the nearest penny.

6.22 Where payment is in arrears the amount due to the landlord is:

☐   the daily rate of personal charge;
☐   multiplied by the number of days in the period before the rent or payment day.

6.23 Where payment is in advance the amount due is:

☐   the daily rate;
☐   multiplied by the days in the period on or after the rent or payment day and prior to the next such day which the landlord estimates the resident will be liable for.

EW Act sch 2   **6.24** If it appears to the landlord that the resident's liability will stop
para 7   before the end of the advance period the amount due must be worked out on the basis of that shorter period if the resident requests it.

S Act s 11   **6.25** For Scottish residents the amount of the contribution is:

☐   the island or regional and district personal charge;
☐   divided by the number of days in the year;
☐   multiplied by the number of days the individual is solely or mainly resident in the premises.

Receipts

EW Act sch 2
para 8
S Act s 11

6.26 The landlord must supply the resident with a receipt as soon as practicable after the resident has made a contribution. In Scotland, and in practice in England and Wales too, the receipt must show the amount paid and the days to which the contributions relate.

EW Act sch 3
para 2

6.27 In England and Wales if the landlord fails to supply a receipt without reasonable excuse the registration officer may impose a penalty of £50.

The resident's right to inspect the landlord's records

EW Act sch 2
EW reg 12

6.28 In England and Wales residents liable to pay contributions may inspect any records their landlord has supplied to the authority or the registration officer.

Over and underpayment of contributions

EW Act sch 2
para 7

6.29 In England and Wales at both the end of each financial year and the end of the resident's liability to make contributions the landlord must as soon as practicable:

☐ work out the contributions payable by the resident;
☐ supply the resident with information on the amount of the liability;
☐ repay any amount overpaid by the resident; and
☐ recover any amount underpaid by the resident.

EW Act s 9
sch 2 para 7

6.30 In the first year of the community charge (1990-91) no contribution is payable for each day that the authority fails to set a personal charge. In future years if the authority fails to inform the landlord of the amount of its personal charge the resident's contribution is worked out on the basis of the old amount until the necessary information is provided. As soon as the information is provided adjustments should be made either by way of the landlord making repayments or the resident making additional payments so that the amounts paid represent the contributions due for the days to which those payments relate.

S Act s 11   **6.31** In Scotland if the resident overpays contributions for any reason and makes a claim to the landlord for the excess payment within 3 months of the overpayment the landlord must repay it.

6.32 It is important to note that unlike the situation that prevails in England and Wales (para. 6.29) a landlord in Scotland is not under an obligation to repay any contribution that has been overpaid. The landlord need only repay if the resident asks for it and that request is made within 3 months of the original overpayment.

Is the landlord liable for the collective charge?

6.33 Where there is a fear that the landlord is asking for contributions when he or she does not have to pay the collective charge the public may confirm or refute this liability by inspecting information held by the authority.

EW reg 11   **6.34** In England and Wales the public may inspect a separate list of buildings which are subject to the charge. This list is created and maintained by the registration officer and kept available for public inspection.

S Act s 20   **6.35** In Scotland the public have the right to inspect the extract from the register which shows the address of premises and the collective charge multiplier for those premises subject to the charge.

Contribution payments are not rent

EW Act sch 2
paras 19,20
S Act s 11   **6.36** Contribution payments are not to be treated as rent or any other consideration for accommodation. Consequently they cannot be subject to any form of rent control or taken by the landlord as rent, and arrears of contributions cannot be recovered as part of any legal action relating to arrears of rent.

CHAPTER 7

Help with paying the community charge

7.1 Individuals may receive help to pay the community charge in 2 ways. This chapter considers:

☐ the transitional relief scheme; and
☐ community charge benefit.

7.2 Certain individuals face a significant additional financial burden as a result of the introduction of the community charge. Some may be helped through the transitional relief schemes which run for 3 years.

Transitional relief (TR) schemes

7.3 These exist in England, Wales and Scotland. Each scheme is different. In Wales transitional relief is deducted automatically from the amount that chargepayers living in specific communities have to pay. The Scottish scheme operates retrospectively for 1989-90. At the time of writing no further details are available on the Scottish scheme. The details of the English scheme are described below.

Entitlement

EW Act s 13A   **7.4** Transitional relief (TR) is available for:
SI 1990 No.2

☐ former rate payers and partners if the government's assumed community charge is substantially higher than their previous rates bill; and
☐ people who were pensioners on or before 1 April 1990, and people with disabilities who were not ratepayers or the partners of ratepayers.

7.5 Women, 60 and over, and men 65 and over, count as pensioners. A person counts as disabled if he or she satisfies the condition for the community charge benefit disability premium (Table 7.3).

7.6 Only those people entered on the register as liable for the personal community charge on 31 March 1990 are eligible for TR. TR is not available in respect of the standard or collective charge or contributions paid by residents to a landlord liable for the collective charge.

7.7 People who are not on the register on 31 March 1990 but who are subsequently entered as being liable from that date, are eligible for relief unless they:

☐ have not properly complied with the statutory duties to provide information to the registration officer; or

☐ were not on the register at 31 March 1990 due to a failure to provide the required information unless there is good cause for that failure.

7.8 Exempt individuals (Chapter 3) are not entitled to TR. Their exclusion from the register means that they do not effect the calculation of TR (Table 7.1).

Application for TR

7.9 Former ratepayers and the partners of former ratepayers do not have to apply for TR – it is awarded automatically. Pensioners and the disabled must apply to the authority. Authorities may specify a cut-off date by which applications for transitional relief must be made. This must be 1 October 1990 or a later date allowed by the authority.

The calculation of TR

7.10 Different TR calculations are carried out for:

☐ former ratepayers and the partners of former ratepayers; and
☐ pensioners and the disabled.

TR for former ratepayers and partners

7.11 The amount of relief is dependent upon:

☐ the assumed community charge in the individual area for 1990-91; and

☐ the assumed rates bill for 1989-90 for the property the individual is living in on 31 March 1990.

7.12 The exact amount of relief to which the individual is entitled depends upon the number of people living in the property as shown in Table 7.1.

Table 7.1

TR FOR FORMER RATEPAYERS AND THEIR PARTNERS

Where there is one chargepayer in occupation:

☐ TR = 1990-91 assumed community charge;
☐ minus the assumed rates bill for the property;
☐ plus £156.

Where there are two chargepayers in occupation:

☐ TR = (2 × 1990-91 assumed community charge)
☐ minus (the assumed rates bill for the property plus £156)
☐ divided by 2.

Where there are more than two chargepayers in occupation:

☐ TR = (2 × 1990-91 assumed community charge);
☐ minus (the assumed rates bill for the property plus £156);
☐ divided by the number of people eligible for TR.

7.13 The assumed personal charge used in the calculation is determined by central government. If the authority's actual charge is above that amount, the difference has to be met by the chargepayer.

The authority's actual charge is used if it is less than the government assumed charge.

7.14 The rates bill used in the calculation is not necessarily the one actually payable on the property concerned in 1989-90. It is an assumed amount based on the rateable value of the property shown in the valuation list on 31 March 1990 multiplied by the average domestic rate poundage, as set by the government.

Examples

The chargepayer is a former ratepayer who is the only occupier of the dwelling. The assumed rates bill for 1989-90 is £160 and the government assumed charge is £380. The actual charge is £395.

☐   TR = £380 − (£160 + £156) = £64

The chargepayer receives TR of £64 which is deducted from the actual community charge bill of £395. Thus the chargepayer has to pay £331 if there is no community charge benefit entitlement. If the chargepayer is also entitled to benefit then the amount of that entitlement is deducted from the community charge figure after the application of TR.

If the actual charge had been £350 then that figure would have been used rather than the government's assumed figure for the charge. The chargepayer's TR would have been:

☐   TR = £350 − (£160 + £156) = £34

The chargepayer, the partner of a former ratepayer, lives in a property with one other chargepayer (wife and husband). The assumed rates bill for 1989-90 is £360 and the government assumed community charge is £320. The actual charge is £365.

☐ $TR = \dfrac{(2 \times £320) - (£360 + £156)}{2} = £62$

The chargepayer receives TR of £62 which is deducted from the actual charge of £365. Thus the chargepayer has to pay £303 if she has no community charge benefit entitlement.

7.15 For full-time students in advanced education, relief is calculated on the full personal charge but the student is only entitled to 20 per cent of the amount.

Pensioners and people with disabilities

7.16 Pensioners and people with disabilities are protected against assumed personal charges greater than £156. Their TR is:

☐ assumed personal charge – £156.

Example

A pensioner lives with her adult son and his partner. Her son was previously responsible for the rates on his property. The government assumed community charge is £320. The authority's actual community charge is £350.

☐ TR = £320 - £156 = £164

The chargepayer is entitled to TR of £164. If not entitled to community charge benefit she must pay a community charge of £186 (i.e. the actual charge minus the TR). Any benefit entitlement would reduce this amount further.

TR in future years

7.17 There is no reassessment of entitlement in later years. Transitional relief is withdrawn as follows:

☐ 1991-92 – relief awarded in 1990-91 is reduced by £13.
☐ 1992-93 – relief entitlement in 1991-92 is reduced by £13.
☐ 1993-94 – no relief is paid.

Effect of TR on community charge benefit (CCB)

7.18 CCB is based on the claimant's reduced personal charge liability. Thus the TR must be calculated first.

BETTER OFF PROBLEM

SI 1990
No.2

7.19 In certain cases the award of TR is disadvantageous for claimants. Where the claimant receives a small amount of CCB the award of TR may remove all entitlement making the chargepayer worse off. In such cases the authority should withhold TR and explain the reason to the claimant. Authorities must also inform such claimants that if they cease to be entitled to CCB they are entitled to have the TR reinstated. Where a claimant applies for CCB after receiving a bill net of relief the authority must withdraw relief before calculating CCB if this produces the best result for the claimant.

Payment of TR

7.20 The relief is paid by a reduction in the individual's community charge. Chargepayers should receive community charge bills which take into account their relief under the scheme.

End of relief

7.21 Entitlement to relief ceases before the end of the 3-year period if the chargepayer:

☐   makes a voluntary move; or
☐   ceases to be subject to the community charge he or she was liable for on 1 April 1990 for any other reason.

7.22 If the chargepayer makes an involuntary move, e.g. a housing authority moves him or her to undertake extensive repair or improvement to the home, or the property is damaged or destroyed by fire or flood, or the subject of compulsory purchase, TR continues provided the chargepayer remains in the authority's area.

7.23 Where someone moves or dies after 1 April 1990 leaving other people in the property their entitlement to relief is unchanged.

Appeals

7.24 Chargepayers who disagree with a decision on TR may make representations to the authority and take the matter further if they are still not satisfied with an appeal to the authority's housing benefit/community charge benefit review board. There is no right of appeal to a Valuation and Community Charge Tribunal (VCCT) on any matters relating solely to TR.

Subsidy for authorities

7.25 Central government will pay authorities:

☐ a specific grant of 100 per cent of the income foregone via TR payments; and

☐ 100 per cent of the reasonable costs of setting-up and administering the scheme.

Community charge benefit (CCB)

EW Act s 135
sch 10

7.26 Community charge benefit (CCB) is a scheme administered by authorities. It helps certain people on low incomes pay their community charge or contributions. Authorities should seek to maximise the number of successful CCB claims. The achievement of such a goal not only reduces the cost of the community charge to low income individuals, it also minimises the authority's own collection costs and the scope for arrears. The scheme operates throughout Great Britain from 1 April 1990. It replaces the community charge rebate scheme that operated in Scotland in 1989-90 and the rate rebate scheme which operated in England and Wales. It retains many of the features of those schemes.

7.27 The details of the CCB scheme are contained in SI 1989 No. 1321 – Community Charge Benefits (General) Regulations; and the transitional arrangements in SI 1989 No. 1322 – Community Charge Benefits (Transitional) Order. This section provides an overview of the main features of the CCB scheme. For an explanation of the full details see *Guide to Housing Benefit and Community Charge Benefit 1990-91* by Martin Ward and John Zebedee.

Who can claim CCB?

7.28 A person can get CCB if he or she has to pay:

☐ a personal charge; or
☐ contributions to a landlord who is liable for the collective charge.

7.29 People from abroad who are liable for the personal charge or contributions are not excluded from claiming CCB on the grounds that they are citizens of a foreign country or that they have been permitted to enter the UK on limited leave. Claims for CCB, unlike those for housing benefit, income support, or family credit, do not count as having 'recourse to public funds' under the immigration rules.

7.30 Student who only have to pay 20 per cent of the charge cannot get CCB. Also CCB cannot be paid to help with the payment of a standard charge or the collective charge paid by certain landlords.

7.31 Only one claim is required from a couple where the claimant:

☐ is married and lives in the same house as his or her husband or wife; or
☐ lives with a partner of the opposite sex as husband and wife.

Other members of a household, e.g. an adult son or daughter or an elderly parent, must make their own claims.

7.32 Where a claimant is liable for both a personal and a collective charge contribution – which may be the case in England and Wales (para. 6.5) but not Scotland (para. 6.9) – CCB can be paid on both amounts. A separate claim has to be made for each amount.

How to claim CCB

PRIOR TO 1 APRIL 1990

7.33 Claims for CCB could be made before 1 April 1990. They have effect from that date.

CLAIMANT IN RECEIPT OF HOUSING BENEFIT

7.34 In England and Wales where the claimant was already receiving housing benefit for rates or rent the need for a new claim form could be waived by the authority. Alternatively the authority could contact the claimant asking for a new CCB claim form to be completed and returned. In Scotland claimants in receipt of community charge rebate did not need to make a separate claim for CCB unless requested to do so by the authority.

CLAIMANT IN RECEIPT OF INCOME SUPPORT BUT NOT HOUSING BENEFIT

7.35 If the claimant was not on housing benefit but was in receipt of income support the local office of the DSS should have sent out a CCB claim form asking for it to be completed and returned. The DSS should then have sent it to the authority with form NHB2 stating whether or not the claimant was receiving income support. .

INDIVIDUAL NOT ON INCOME SUPPORT OR HOUSING BENEFIT

7.36 Where potential CCB claimants were not in receipt of either housing benefit or income support they should have asked the authority for a claim form. This should have been completed and returned to the authority.

AFTER 1 APRIL 1990

7.37 A claim may be made direct to the authority on its own claim form or via the local office of the DSS in conjunction with a claim for income support.

7.38 Income support claimants may claim CCB by completing the combined housing benefit and CCB claim form (NHB1) in the appropriate income support claim form (B1 – unemployed, A1 – sick/disabled/ single parents, SP1 – pensioners). The DSS assesses income support and sends the NHB1 to the authority with a decision notice that informs the authority as to whether or not, and from what date, the claimant is entitled to income support. The authority requests any further information needed from the claimant and assesses CCB entitlement.

Information needed for working out CCB

7.39 The following information is required to work out the claimant's and any partner's CCB entitlement. It is acquired from the completed claim form, notification from the DSS, and the authority's own records:

☐ the claimant's (and partner's) contributions or personal charge before any discounts have been applied but after any transitional relief (TR) has been deducted; and

☐ whether the claimant is getting income support.

7.40 If the claimant or partner is not getting income support then the following additional information is also needed:

☐ the composition of the claimant's household;

☐ the claimant's applicable amount;

☐ the amount of capital belonging to the claimant and any partner minus disregarded capital;

☐ the claimant (and partner's) net income minus disregarded income.

THE CLAIMANT'S HOUSEHOLD

7.41 This includes the applicant and any partner – i.e. husband and wife or a couple 'living together as husband and wife' and any children (under 16) or young person (16–18 years old for whom child benefit is payable) the claimant is responsible for.

CAPITAL

7.42 The capital (e.g. money in a bank account, property, etc) of the applicant and any partner is taken into account if it is between £3,000 and £8,000. Certain capital items, however, are disregarded, e.g.

☐ the claimant's home and certain other property;

☐ personal possessions;

☐ arrears of: CCB, housing benefit, attendance allowance, mobility allowance, income support and family credit; but only for 52 weeks.

7.43 Capital which counts for CCB purposes is assumed to provide the claimant with £1 of income for each £250, between £3,000 and £8,000. If the claimant has more then £8,000 capital, no CCB is payable.

INCOME

7.44 If the claimant or partner has earned income this is taken into account net of any tax, class 1 national insurance contributions and 50 per cent of any contributions towards a pension.

7.45 Certain amounts of earned income is disregarded. The main disregards are:

☐ £15 for lone parents and those with a disability or severe disability premium (This increases to £25 for lone parents from October 1990);
☐ £10 for couples (other than above);
☐ £5 for single claimants (other than above).

7.46 Most unearned income, such as pensions, child benefit, family credit and maintenance payments, is taken into account. Some items of unearned income are disregarded. The main disregards are:

☐ attendance and mobility allowance, mobility supplements and housing benefit;
☐ income in kind;
☐ £10 of war disablement pension or war widows pension.

The authority may resolve to disregard more or all of a war pension under a local scheme and the rules on these disregards are likely to change further by 1 April 1990.

APPLICABLE AMOUNT

7.47 The claimant's needs are measured by applicable amounts (Table 7.2). These are supposed to reflect the day to day living needs of the applicant and any family members.

7.48 The applicable amount is made up of:

☐ personal allowances – which vary according to age and with different amount for single people, lone parents and couples;
☐ dependants' allowances for each child and young person – varying according to 4 age bands;
☐ premiums – to meet the additional needs of the groups described in Table 7.3.

Table 7.2

APPLICABLE AMOUNTS 1990 – 91

Personal Allowances

Single claimant:	
aged under 25	£28.80
aged 25 or over	£36.70
Lone parent:	
aged 18 or over	£36.70
Couple:	
at least one aged 18 or over	£57.60

Dependant's allowances for each child/young person who does not have capital over £3,000:

aged under 11	£12.35
aged 11 to 15 inclusive	£18.25
aged 16 or 17	£21.90
aged 18	£28.80

Premiums

A claimant is awarded any of the following which apply:

Family premium	£7.35
Disabled child premium	£15.40
Severe disability premium:	
single claimant or lone parent	£28.20
couple (single rate)	£28.20
couple (double rate)	£56.40

Plus the highest of any of the following which apply:

Lone parent premium	£9.70
Pensioner premium:	
single claimant	£11.80
couple	£17.95

Table 7.2, continued	
Enhanced pensioner premium:	
single claimant	£14.40
couple	£21.60
Higher pensioner premium:	
single claimant	£17.05
couple	£24.25
Disability premium:	
single claimant or lone parent	£15.40
couple	£22.10
Carer's premium	£10.00
(available from October 1990)	

Table 7.3

PREMIUMS AND ENTITLEMENT CONDITIONS

Premium	Condition
☐ Family premium	Claimant is responsible for a child or young person.
☐ Lone parent premium	Claimant has no partner and is responsible for a child or young person.
☐ Disabled child premium	Child or young person who does not have capital over £3,000 and receives attendance or mobility allowance, or is registered blind.
☐ Disability premium	Claimant or partner receives attendance, mobility or severe disablement allowance, mobility supplement or invalidity pension, or has (money from the DSS for) an invalid vehicle, or is registered blind; or the claimant has been incapable of work due to sickness or disability for 28 weeks.
☐ Severely disabled premium	Claimant receives attendance allowance and no-one receives invalid care allowance to look after him or her and no adult in the house is able to care for the claimant. The couple rate is only payable if all the above applies to both the claimant and partner.
☐ Pensioner premium	Claimant or partner is aged 60 or over.
☐ Enhanced pensioner premium	Claimant or partner is aged 75 or over.
☐ Higher pensioner premium	Claimant or partner is aged 80 or over; or aged 60 or over and satisfies the condition for disability premium.
☐ Carer's premium[1]	Claimant or partner receives invalid care allowance.

1. This premium is available from October 1990.

PROOF

7.49 The claimant must supply any proof, e.g., of capital or income, as may be reasonably required by the authority.

Working out CCB

7.50 Community charge is an individual liability but couples are assessed jointly for CCB. In most cases couples have the same charge liability. In these cases their charge liabilities are combined for the assessment of CCB. This is not the case where the claimant or partner is a full-time student. In such cases the student's charge liability is ignored but his or her needs and resources are included with the partner's to work out CCB entitlement.

7.51 Benefit is awarded in proportion to each partner's charge liability. Where the couple are both equally liable for the charge CCB is divided equally between them. In certain cases, however, a couple are not both equally liable for the charge, e.g. when one is a full-time student, under 18, or exempt. In these cases CCB entitlement is awarded to the partner that has to pay the full charge.

CLAIMANT ON INCOME SUPPORT

7.52 Where the claimant is on income support the maximum benefit is 80 per cent of the community charge or collective contribution. The community water charge payable in Scotland is not eligible for benefit. All calculations are based on weekly (not annual) liability.

Examples

A resident in a hostel subject to the collective community charge pays her landlord a collective community charge contribution of £4.50 per week. The resident is in receipt of income support. Her CCB entitlement is £3.60

i.e. £4.50 × 80% = £3.60

The chargepayer lives with a partner as husband and wife. Both are individually liable for a personal charge of £6.50 per week. The claimant is in receipt of income support. Their individual CCB entitlement is £5.20.

£6.50 + £6.50 = £13.00
£13.00 × 80% = £10.40
£10.40 ÷ 2 = £5.20

CLAIMANT NOT ON INCOME SUPPORT

7.53 Where the claimant is not on income support the net income after any disregards is compared with the relevant applicable amount. If the claimant's income is:

☐ at, or below, the applicable amount, the maximum CCB – 80 per cent of the personal charge or contribution – is payable;
☐ above the applicable amount, then for every £1 above that amount the authority deduct 15p off the maximum benefit.

7.54 The resulting sum, as long as it is at or above the minimum payment of 50p per claim, is the amount of benefit awarded.

Examples

The claimant is a single pensioner aged 67 with a state pension of £46.90 per week and savings which have reduced over a number of years to £3,010. The personal charge is £450. The weekly CCB entitlement is calculated as follows:

☐ weekly personal charge is £8.61 (i.e. £450 ÷ 365 × 7);
☐ maximum CCB = £6.89 (i.e. £8.61 × 80%);
☐ income for CCB = £47.90 (£46.90 from pensions plus £1 assumed income from savings);
☐ applicable amount = £48.50 (personal allowance for a claimant aged 25 or over of £36.70, plus pensioner premium of £11.80 + 36.70);
☐ income is below applicable amount therefore the claimant's CCB = £6.89 (maximum benefit entitlement).

The claimant is also potentially entitled to a small amount of income support.

The claimant is a single person, aged 35, with no capital and net earnings of £55 per week. The personal charge is £450. The weekly CCB entitlement is calculated as follows:

☐ weekly personal charge is £8.61 per week;
☐ maximum CCB = £6.89 (i.e. £8.61 × 80%);
☐ income for CCB = £50 (i.e. net earnings of £55 per week minus earned income disregard of £5);
☐ applicable amount = £36.70 (personal allowance for single claimant aged 25 or over, no dependants allowance or premiums);
☐ income exceeds the applicable amount (£50 – £36.70) by £13.30;
☐ the maximum CCB is reduced by £2.00 (i.e. £13.30 × 15%);
☐ CCB = £4.89 (i.e. the maximum benefit of £6.89 less £2.00 calculated as above).

A couple, aged 35 and 32, have two children aged 4 and 7. The couple have a total net income of £175 per week (including child benefit of £14.50 which counts in full). The personal charge is £450.

Examples, continued

☐ weekly personal charge is £8.63 per week for each partner, i.e. £17.26 in total;
☐ maximum CCB = £13.81 (i.e. £17.26 × 80%);
☐ income for CCB = £165 (total net income of £175 per week minus earned income disregard of £10);
☐ applicable amount = £89.65 (personal allowance for couple at least one aged 18 is £57.60, plus dependants allowance £24.70 (i.e. 12.35 × 2), plus family premium of £7.35);
☐ income exceeds the applicable amount by £75.35 (i.e. £165 − £89.65);
☐ the maximum CCB is reduced by £11.30 (i.e. £75.35 × 15%);
☐ CCB = £2.51 (i.e. the maximum benefit of £13.81 less £11.30 calculated as above);
☐ each partner receives CCB of £1.26 (i.e. £2.51 ÷ 2).

Additional benefit in exceptional circumstances

7.55 The claimant may be awarded additional benefit if his or her circumstances are exceptional. This is a wide discretionary power and there are no pre-set rules as to what circumstances may be considered exceptional. CCB may not be increased by more than the maximum CCB figure – 80 per cent of full liability. Total expenditure by the authority under this power is cash limited.

Start of claim and backdating

7.56 CCB usually starts from the Monday after the claim form arrives at either the DSS or authority benefit office. Claims made within 56 days of either 1 April 1990 or the date on which the claimant receives the first community charge bill (where this is later) may be treated as having been made on 1 April 1990. This is only the case, however, where the claimant:

☐   is liable for a charge on 1 April 1990; and

☐   has not attempted to avoid registration.

7.57 After this period claims may only be backdated for up to 52 weeks where the claimant shows continuous good cause for not claiming earlier. The authority has no discretion on this matter. If the claimant can show continuous good cause then the authority must backdate. However, it suffers a subsidy penalty imposed by central government and may need to be pressed to backdate the claim.

Changes of circumstance and end of claim

7.58 CCB is revised if any of the elements that are used in working out entitlement change, e.g. entitlement to income support, the amount of earnings or capital, the make-up of the claimant's household. The claimant has a duty to advise the authority of any relevant changes in his or her circumstances. CCB may last for up to 60 weeks but claimants are normally asked to submit a new claim at the end of the financial year or earlier in certain circumstances.

Help via the income support personal allowance?

7.59 The Government's aim in making everyone who is liable for the charge pay a minimum 20 per cent is to help promote local accountability. Most people now have a direct financial interest in their authority's spending policies. For those receiving income support their personal allowance includes an element to reflect 20 per cent of the national average community charge. Some gain and some lose depending upon the level of charge set by their authority. Furthermore, though the personal allowances include an element to meet community charge liability the total allowances may be inadequate to meet the claimant's weekly needs.

Notification, payment and overpayment

7.60 The authority should normally determine and notify the claimant of the results of the CCB claim within 14 days of receiving all the information it requires.

7.61 CCB is normally paid straight into the claimant's community charge account. The claimant should receive a revised community charge bill with the total reduced by the amount of the rebate. Claimants paying contributions to a landlord liable for the collective charge should receive their first payment within 7 days. Payment may be by way of cash, cheque, giro, voucher or (if the claimant agrees) direct to the landlord's collective charge account.

7.62 Overpaid CCB (referred to as excess benefit) may be recovered unless it was due to an error by the authority or DSS and the claimant could not have realised that the overpayment occurred at the time of payment. The authority may seek to recover excess benefit by:

☐ requiring direct payment from the claimant or partner;

☐ adding an amount to the claimant's community charge bill;

☐ requesting the local office of the DSS to recover the excess from certain benefits, e.g. income support and family credit.

7.63 Excess CCB cannot be recovered from a claimant's housing benefit. In Scotland recoverable overpayments of community charge rebate may be recovered from community charge benefit entitlement.

Further information, representation and review

7.64 If the claimant requests it, the authority must supply a written explanation of their determinations relating to the claim. Where the claimant disagrees with the way the authority has worked out the CCB entitlement he or she has 6 weeks from the date of notification to request the authority to hold an internal review of the claim. This 6-week period is in addition to any time taken by the authority to supply a written explanation of its determinations. If the claimant is still not satisfied the matter must go to the authority's Review Board. The Review Board's decision is final unless challenged by judicial review. A review board decision does not establish a precedent.

CHAPTER 8

Collection of information

8.1 This chapter is concerned with the information needed about people who have to pay the community charge. It covers:

- ☐ the community charge register;
- ☐ the duties of the registration officer;
- ☐ when register entries are made and backdated; and
- ☐ how information is obtained and who must provide it.

The community charge register

EW Act ss 6,31
S Act s 13
S SI 1989
No.1539

8.2 The community charge register contains details of all the community charge contributions due to the authority. Its purpose it to provide a regularly updated list of each person who is subject to any personal, standard or collective community charge in the area.

S SI 1989
No.1539

8.3 In probably all authorities, the register is held on computer. It must be printed out from time to time, and each entry is notified to the chargepayer concerned. Unless the chargepayer successfully appeals against the entry (Chapter 12), the information contained in it is used to raise his or her community charge bill. Chapter 9 gives further information about how chargepayers, members of the public and others can find out what information is held.

8.4 A separate register is held by each authority responsible for raising community charges (paras 1.20–23); and in Scotland registers for regional councils must be divided into separate parts coinciding with district council areas.

THE CONTENTS OF THE REGISTER

EW Act ss 6,31
S Act s 13
S SI 1988
No.1539

8.5 Everyone who has to pay any community charge appears on the register. If someone has to pay more than one charge (e.g. a personal charge and a collective charge), a separate entry is made for each. Table 8.1 shows exactly what information must be contained in the register (though registers need not be kept in the order shown there).

8.6 The law provides for more information to be shown in registers in Scotland than in those in England and Wales. This is partly because of differences in the structure of the community charge scheme, and partly because of differences of emphasis between the 2 systems about what legally forms part of the register and what additional information is kept by the authority as an administrative back-up (para. 8.7).

Table 8.1

THE CONTENTS OF THE COMMUNITY CHARGE REGISTER

NAME	The name of everyone liable to pay any of the community charges in the area. This includes ordinary individuals and, e.g., companies.
COMMUNITY CHARGE	Whether the community charge due is a personal, standard or collective charge.
ADDRESS(ES)	In the case of a personal charge, the address (or other identifying description) of the person's sole or main residence. In the case of a standard or collective charge, the address of the property for which the charge arises and, if different, the person's current residential address (or, in the case of a company, the company's registered office).
STUDENT	In the case of a personal charge, whether the person qualifies for the student reduction (para. 2.10).
STANDARD COMMUNITY CHARGE CLASS	In the case of a standard charge, the class into which the property falls for the purpose of determining the multiplier (para. 4.19). (At the time of writing, the law in Scotland has not been amended to include this in the contents of the register.)
DATE(S) OF LIABILITY	The date the entry has effect in beginning, changing or ending the person's liability.

Additional information included in Scotland

DATE OF BIRTH	The date of birth of the person.
DISTRICT	In the case of registers for regional councils, the appropriate district.
FURTHER STANDARD AND COLLECTIVE COMMUNITY CHARGE DETAILS	In the case of a collective charge, the multiplier for the property (para. 5.27). In the case of a standard or collective charge, whether the person is liable because of being an owner or a tenant, and the extent (if any) to which joint and several liability exists with any other owner or tenant of the property (para. 10.79).
WATER	Whether the person is also liable to pay the corresponding community water charge.
DATE OF MAKING	The date on which the entry or most recent amendment was actually made (as opposed to the date it is effective).

OTHER INFORMATION

EW Act s 6
S Act s 13

8.7 Only the information shown in the table is included in the register. However, authorities usually keep some additional information as an administrative back-up. This cannot be obtained as though it were required for the register itself (i.e. the rules in paras 8.19 onwards do not apply). In particular, the register does not contain any information about:

☐ people who are exempt from personal charges;
☐ people liable to pay their landlords collective (and, in Scotland, standard) community charge contributions (paras 4.5, 6.4);
☐ relationships between people (e.g. in the case of potential joint and several liability between couples);
☐ in England and Wales, dates of birth;
☐ in England and Wales, the date an entry is made (as opposed to the effective date).

DATES OF BIRTH

8.8 In England and Wales, dates of birth are not contained in registers. The practice note, *The Community Charges Register*, (PN No. 3, paras 3.4–5) suggests that they should not normally be required at all by the registration officer, but may be necessary in the case of young people who will reach their 18th birthday during the course of the year, or when there are 2 people with the same name living at the same address.

The registration officer

EW Act s 26
S Act s 12

8.9 Responsibility for compiling and maintaining the register lies with the community charge registration officer. In England and Wales, this is the authority's chief finance officer; in Scotland, the regional or islands assessor.

EW Act s 26
S Act s 12

8.10 In legal terms, the registration officer's duties are independent of the authority itself. The registration officer is responsible for the community charge register, whereas the authority is responsible for the billing and collection of charges. In Scotland, the authority may appoint deputy registration officers, with all the powers and duties of the registration officer. In England and Wales, the registration officer may authorise others to act on his or her behalf, but may not delegate his or her functions (PN No. 3, para. 1.5). In practice some authorities have one department responsible for registration and another for billing and collection. Others combine these functions in a single department.

EW Act ss 26–28
S Act s 12

8.11 The authority must provide the registration officer with the staff, accommodation and other resources necessary for his or her duties. In England and Wales, the Secretary of State has reserve powers to ensure that adequate resources are provided and that the register is sufficiently comprehensive; including the right to require specific things to be done.

Making and backdating entries

EW Act s 6
S Act s 14
S SI 1988
No.1539

8.12 The first community charge registers should have been compiled in Scotland by 1 October 1988, and in England and Wales by 1 December 1989. From then onwards, registers must be kept up to date.

DATE OF ENTRIES

EW Act ss 8,31
S Act s 15

8.13 Entries and amendments to entries (including entries showing the end of liability for a charge) may be made in the register on, before or after the date they take effect. Entries may therefore be anticipated or backdated. For example, an entry might be anticipated in the case of someone whose 18th birthday falls within the current financial year.

BACKDATING ENTRIES AND AMENDMENTS

EW Act s 8
S Act s 15

8.14 Although register entries must show the exact date when a person's liability for a charge begins, changes or ends (no matter how long ago), there is in practice a 2-year limit to backdating. The earliest date an entry, amendment or deletion can take effect is 2 years before the date on which it is made. The following examples illustrate how this works.

8.15 The backdating rules apply regardless of why the delay occurred, whether as a result of administrative error or the fault of the person concerned. In certain cases, however, a person who avoids paying a community charge may be liable to pay a penalty or surcharge (Chapter 11).

Examples

BACKDATING

A man moves into an authority's area on 1 May 1990. Much later, an entry is made in the authority's register showing him as subject to a personal charge from that date.

If the entry is made on 1 February 1992, it takes effect from 1 May 1990: he has to pay a personal charge back to that date.

If the entry is made on 1 June 1992, he only has to pay a personal charge from 1 June 1990 inclusive (2 years before).

A woman has been on an authority's register as subject to a personal charge since 15 June 1990. Much later, the entry is amended to show her as having been exempt from that date.

If the entry is amended on or before 15 June 1992, it takes effect from 15 June 1990: she can recover the charge she has paid.

If the entry is made on 1 April 1993, it only takes effect from 2 years before. She can only recover the charge she has paid for the period from 1 April 1991 inclusive.

STUDENTS

8.16 In England and Wales only, there is some doubt about whether the 2-year backdating limitation applies in relation to someone who becomes eligible or ceases to qualify, for the student reduction (para. 2.10) during a period whilst he or she is on an authority's register. This is because the English and Welsh law, as it stands at the time of writing, does not apply the limitation to cases of amendments to entries with the same rigour as the Scottish law does. For example, if someone has appeared on a register as subject to a personal charge, and an amendment is made recognising him or her as a student, there appears to be no limit to how far back he or she can recover the resultant overpayment of community charge.

COLLECTIVE COMMUNITY CHARGE MULTIPLIERS

S Act s 15   **8.17** In Scotland, there is an additional restriction. No amendment of the collective community charge multiplier (Chapter 5) may take effect until 3 months after the amending entry is made or takes effect, whichever is later; and no more than one such amendment may take effect in any one financial year. However, this limitation does not apply to the correction of a clerical or typographical error.

DELETING ENTRIES

EW Act s 8   **8.18** Entries may be removed from the register at any time after 2
S Act s 15   years have passed since the person was shown as ceasing to be subject to the charge concerned. Until then, old records must remain on the register. The practice note (PN No. 3, paras 3.8–9) suggests that entries should be removed on a regular basis, in order to keep the register up to date; and that entries which have been removed should remain available in a separate archive.

Obtaining information

EW Act ss 6,22   **8.19** The registration officer is under a duty to take reasonable steps
S Act s 17   to obtain information needed to compile and maintain the register, and is given various powers to assist with this. These powers are described below, and are summarised in Table 8.2.

Table 8.2

PROVIDING INFORMATION TO THE REGISTRATION OFFICER

Who must provide information	What information must be provided
Anyone the registration officer designates as 'responsible person' for a property.	Information to establish whether anyone is subject to any community charge by virtue of that property.
Anyone the registration officer believes may be subject to a community charge.	Information to establish whether he or she is subject to any community charge.
Anyone whose details are not recorded, or are recorded wrongly, in the register.	That his or her entry is missing, or incorrect; or the circumstances which have changed.
Educational establishments.	The names and term-time addresses of their full-time students.
Other authority departments, electoral registration officers, and registration officers for other authorities.	Various information – with certain restrictions.
Registrars of births and deaths.	Details of deaths in the area.
Department of Social Security local offices. *This is a discretionary duty only.*	Names and addresses of people (and their partners) aged 18 or over on income support who have not claimed community charge benefit.

8.20 The registration officer may only insist that someone provides information if he or she has the power to do so, and the information is necessary for the register (paras 8.5–6). People who fail to provide such information, or who provide false information, may be subject to penalties or surcharges (Chapter 11). The practice note, *The Community Charge Canvass*, points out that people are not required to provide information to a registration officer 'if they can prove that [he or she] does not reasonably need that information to carry out [his or her] statutory functions'. Registration officers should not make requests for additional information 'without making it quite clear that people do not have to respond to them, and that no penalty can be imposed if they do not' (PN No. 8, paras. 3.2, 3.6).

DUTIES OF RESPONSIBLE PERSONS

EW Act sch 2
EW reg 4
S Act s 17

8.21 The registration officer's principle method of obtaining information is by designating a 'responsible person' for each property in the authority's area (including, where appropriate, mobile homes and houseboats as well as ordinary buildings). The registration officer may then require that person to provide information needed for the purpose of considering whether anyone is, has been, or is about to become, subject to any of the community charges by virtue of that property.

S SI 1988
No.1539

8.22 In Scotland, a full canvass must take place each financial year, requesting information from responsible persons for every property in the authority's area. In England and Wales, registration officers may choose to do this, or to vary the frequency of canvasses. Some authorities, for example, plan to do this every other year. In both cases, registration officers may also request information from responsible persons on a one-off basis at any time (if they believe their records for certain addresses may be out of date).

EW reg 4
S SI 1988
No.1539

8.23 The registration officer must first send a written notice to the responsible person, requesting the information needed. This may be known as a community charge registration form or inquiry form, or by some other name, and may be accompanied by a covering letter. In Scotland, its contents are laid down by regulations, as are the contents of a supplementary form to be used when the registration officer requires additional information or evidence. The initial form in Scotland includes notes, warnings, and questions about:

☐   the address of the property;
☐   details of the water supply;
☐   any or all responsible persons and any other residents;
☐   any full-time students;
☐   anyone who may be exempt from a personal charge; and
☐   possible liability for a standard charge.

8.24 In England and Wales the contents of the form (and of any follow-up form used) are left to the discretion of individual registration officers. The practice note (PN No. 8, para. 2.8 and section 4) provides a model form and advises that forms should:

☐   be easy to understand;
☐   contain clear guidance on the purpose of the form and its completion, both in English and, where appropriate, in other languages;
☐   contain information about exemptions from the community charge;
☐   provide details of where help can be obtained in completing the form;
☐   be designed for convenient computer input; and
☐   clearly spell out the legal duties of responsible persons and the possible penalties which may arise.

EW reg 4
S SI 1988
No.1539

8.25 The responsible person must provide the information requested, so long as it is within his or her possession or control, within 21 days of the date when the request for information is made. In Scotland this begins with the day the registration officer sends the form, posts it or delivers it by hand; and the information must be provided by filling in the supplied form (along with any evidence requested). In England and Wales, the practice note advises that the 21-day limit should be interpreted as running from the date when the request reaches the individual and that, in cases where it is sent by post, this should be assumed to be the date when it would arrive in the normal course of post (PN No. 8, para. 3.7). The information may be supplied by filling in the form or in some other fashion: the law in England and Wales contains no requirement for the information to be supplied in writing.

WHO IS A RESPONSIBLE PERSON IN ENGLAND AND WALES?

EW reg 4   **8.26** In England and Wales, the registration officer decides who is to be a responsible person for any property, and this can change from time to time. The only restriction is that he or she must be an individual aged 18 or over (e.g. a company cannot be a responsible person, though a company director may be, in his or her individual capacity). The registration officer usually designates an owner, tenant or occupier of the property, but can in principle choose anyone whom he or she considers appropriate. The practice note (PN No. 8, para. 2.7) suggests that the latter might be appropriate if the occupier of a property is unable to provide the information (e.g. because of physical or mental incapacity) but a son or daughter elsewhere can do so. The registration officer can later revoke a designation that someone is a responsible person, but only if he or she neither owns (freehold or leasehold) nor occupies the property concerned.

EW reg 4   **8.27** The registration officer can designate more than one responsible person per property. If he or she designates more than one occupier as a responsible person, once one of the occupiers has supplied the information required, there is no longer any duty on the other occupiers. But any non-occupier (e.g. an owner) who has also been designated as a responsible person continues to have a duty to provide the information requested from him or her.

EW reg 4   **8.28** It is not necessary for the registration officer to address the form by name; it may be directed simply to 'the occupier', and posted to the property or left there. In such a case, anyone who is 'in occupation of the property' becomes a responsible person. What counts as 'occupation' is in this context not defined. It would include anyone actually living at the property, but whether it would include a non-resident owner is unclear. The practice note (PN No. 8, para. 2.6) advises that if there is more than one occupier, they are all responsible persons. In such a case, only one of them need provide the information required. It also suggests that 'it will be a defence for failure to provide information for an individual to prove that he or she has not received the request' (PN No. 8, para. 3.9).

WHO IS A RESPONSIBLE PERSON IN SCOTLAND?

S Act s 17   **8.29** In Scotland, the question of who is a responsible person is defined more precisely as follows (the effect is often similar to that in England and Wales):

☐   if the property is occupied by the owner and/or a tenant: each such owner and tenant;
☐   if the property is occupied by neither the owner nor any tenant: any owner or any (non-occupying) tenant with a lease of 12 months or more;
☐   in all cases, any other person at the registration officer's discretion.

S Act s 17   **8.30** There may be more than one responsible person per property. If there are, they may agree with the registration officer that only one of them will undertake the relevant duties. Otherwise, they must all do so. Someone who is designated as a responsible person for a property need not necessarily be designated as such on the next occasion when a form is sent to that property.

OTHERS WHO MAY BE SUBJECT TO A CHARGE

EW reg 5   **8.31** The registration officer may also require information from
S Act s 18A   anyone else whom he or she reasonably believes is, has been or is about to become, subject to any of the authority's community charges (whether an individual or a company, etc). The person must then supply that information, so long as it is within his or her possession or control, within 21 days of the date when the request was made. In Scotland, the registration officer may set a longer period for this purpose. There is no requirement that the information must be supplied in writing.

MISSING AND INCORRECT REGISTER ENTRIES
AND CHANGES OF CIRCUMSTANCES

EW reg 3   **8.32** In addition to the above rules, everyone has a general duty to
S Act s 18   inform the registration officer if he or she believes:
S SI 1988
No.1539
☐   he or she is, or has been, subject to a community charge, and there is no entry on the register about this;
☐   his or her register entry is incorrect because of an error;
☐   his or her register entry is incorrect because of a change of circumstances.

8.33 This rule is designed principally to deal with people who are omitted from a community charge registration canvass or whose circumstances change. For example, it means that someone who moves into an authority's area should inform the registration officer of this. However, no-one has a duty to report changes of circumstances only affecting other people in the household.

8.34 The duty does not depend upon a request from the registration officer: it is a requirement to volunteer information. In England and Wales, the person must inform the registration officer within 21 days; in Scotland, within one month; though the information need not be supplied in writing. In Scotland, there is also a specific rule requiring the executors to notify the registration officer of the death of anyone on a register within one month.

EDUCATIONAL ESTABLISHMENTS

EW SI 1989
No.443
S Act s 8

8.35 Special rules apply for obtaining information about full-time students who qualify for the student reduction in the personal charge (paras 2.10 onwards). One of the qualifications for obtaining the reduction is that the student has a certificate provided by the educational establishment. In England and Wales, this is the responsibility of the establishment's 'certification officer', who is the person having responsibility for registering students' enrolment. The duty falls on that individual, rather than on the educational establishment. If he or she fails to provide a certificate to a qualifying student, the student may take court action against him or her for breach of statutory duty. In Scotland, the responsibility to provide a certificate falls on the educational establishment as a body, and not on any particular individual within it.

EW SI 1989
No.443
S SI 1989
No.32

8.36 The certificate confirms that the student is attending an appropriate course and contains the student's name and the name of the establishment. In Scotland it also includes the student's date of birth and home and term-time addresses (where these are known) and the name of the course: a fresh certificate must be issued each academic year, within 42 days of the student's registration; no expected end date is given. In England and Wales, the certificate must be issued within 21 days of the start of the student's enrolment, or within 21 days of the date when the start of the course is decided (if later). It covers the whole of the student's course, and gives its start date and expected end date: a revised certificate must be issued if the expected end date changes.

EW SI 1989
No.443
S Act s 8
S SI 1989
No.32
8.37 The registration officer may also request supplementary information from educational establishments. In Scotland, this may be any information relevant to the maintenance of the register. In England and Wales, it is restricted to the names and term-time addresses of all full-time students whose term-time address is in the authority's area. The information must be provided within 21 days, but need not be supplied in writing.

8.38 The practice note (PN No. 23, section 4) advises registration officers in England and Wales to request this information once a year, and points out that some institutions have agreed to supply amendment lists voluntarily during the course of the year. It also gives the Government's view that a certification officer who gave a list of all full-time students at the establishment (regardless of age and address) would be fulfilling this duty, and the local authority associations' view that certification officers are under a duty to select for notification only those students whose addresses are within the registration officer's area (regardless of age). In either case, registration officers are likely to have to sort the list.

AUTHORITIES, ETC

EW Act s 133
EW reg 6
EW SI 1989
No.1371
S Act s 17
S SI 1988
No.1539
S SI 1989
No.1371
8.39 Registration officers in England, Wales and Scotland may require information from any of the following:

☐ any department of their own authority;
☐ any electoral registration officer;
☐ any other registration officer;
☐ any other authority responsible for community charges: i.e. district councils and London boroughs in England and Wales, and regional and islands' councils in Scotland;
☐ any housing body, for Scottish registration officers only: i.e. district councils, Scottish Homes, and new town development corporations;
☐ any precepting authority, for English and Welsh registration officers only (e.g. county councils), but not where the information is obtained in connection with police authority duties.

8.40 It is these rules which enable registration officers to obtain from their own authority information about potential chargepayers from (pre-community charge) domestic rates records, non-domestic rates records, council housing rent records and from the electoral register.

It also enables them to obtain information from records held by libraries, recreation centres and social work sections. On the use of such information, see paras 8.46–47.

8.41 Information may not be supplied if it was obtained from records held as an employer. In Scotland, social work departments may only supply names and addresses from their records. In England and Wales, in all cases, the information which may be supplied is restricted to:

☐ the name of any person;
☐ his or her address;
☐ his or her current or former place of residence; and
☐ the dates when he or she is known or thought to have resided there.

8.42 The exact procedural requirements for the exchange of information vary depending upon whether the registration officer making the request and the person requested are:

☐ both in England or Wales. In this case the request must be in writing, and the information must be supplied within 21 days (but not necessarily in writing); or
☐ one in England or Wales and one in Scotland. In this case, the request need not be in writing, but must be supplied within 21 days in writing; or
☐ both in Scotland. In this case, there are no procedural rules about how and when the information must be requested and supplied.

EW reg 6   **8.43** In England and Wales only, registration officers may also volunteer information to other registration officers (who must also be in England or Wales) if they believe it may assist in their duties.

REGISTRAR OF BIRTHS AND DEATHS

EW Act sch 2   **8.44** The Secretary of State is expected to make regulations providing for registrars of births and deaths, and also the Registrar General in appropriate cases, to notify registration officers of deaths within their area. At the time of writing, the regulations have not been made. In Scotland, deaths must also be notified by executors (para. 8.34).

INFORMATION ABOUT SOCIAL SECURITY

EW SI 1989
No.475
S SI 1989
No.476
8.45 The local office of the DSS informs registration officers of the name and address of every income support recipient who is aged 18 or over, who has not (when the income support award is made) claimed community charge benefit via its office. The DSS also provides the name and address of any partner aged 18 or over (i.e. a husband or wife or someone living with the claimant as husband or wife). This rule applies from 1 April 1990, and is designed to ensure that someone who claims income support cannot evade paying a community charge simply by failing to return a community charge benefit claim form with his or her income support claim form. (The procedure is described in para. 7.38.) Prior to 1 April 1990, the DSS informed English and Welsh registration officers where the person had not claimed housing benefit and Scottish registration officers where the person had not claimed community charge rebate.

USE OF THE REGISTRATION OFFICER'S POWERS

8.46 The practice note, *Data Protection and the Community Charge*, provides guidance on which information should be required by the registration officer and how it should be used. It advises that 'only the minimum amount of information necessary for the statutory functions of the [registration officer and authority] should be accessed, collected or held'; and that 'although the Data Protection Act 1984 is limited in its application to community charge systems, it is important that [registration officers and authorities] recognise and take account of the principles of good data protection practice which the Act embodies' (PN No. 4, introduction and para. 2.1).

8.47 The practice note advises that information should only be sought from other departments of the authority, or from other authorities and organisations, as a back-up to other sources (such as the right to obtain information from responsible persons). It points out that some sources, such as social work and housing departments, are more sensitive than others in terms of confidentiality and privacy, and may well feel that the provision of even name and address to the registration officer may deter people in need from applying for assistance. The registration officer should, wherever possible, go to less sensitive sources first; and may wish to balance the concerns of such departments against the marginal benefit to him or her of the information. Any such information actually collected and held should be deleted as soon as it has been used. If there is a possibility that information held for another purpose will be disclosed to the registration officer, then wherever possible the individuals concerned should be informed that this might be the case (PN No. 4, introduction).

CHAPTER 9

Provision and inspection of information

9.1 This chapter considers the rights of the following to be provided with, or to inspect, information related to the community charge:

☐ the chargepayer;
☐ the general public; and
☐ various public officials.

9.2 The chargepayer has a right to be provided with a copy of his or her register entry, to inspect that entry and to obtain additional copies. The general public has a right to inspect an extract of the addresses and names held on the register. The chargepayer's name may be excluded from that extract where there is a threat of violence. The public have a right to know which properties are subject to the collective charge. In England and Wales the individual resident in property subject to the collective charge has a right to inspect a copy of any records submitted to the registration officer by his or her landlord.

The registration officer's duty to provide chargepayers with a copy of the information held on them

EW Act sch 2
para 11
EW reg 9
S SI 1988
No.1539 reg 8
schs 2,3

9.3 Whenever there is a new entry in the register or an amendment to an entry, the registration officer must send the chargepayer a free copy of that new or amended entry. In England and Wales this must be done as soon as reasonably practicable after it is made. In Scotland it must be done within 28 days. It must also be accompanied by notification that identifies the effect of the entry or amendment and the chargepayer's appeal rights, duty to report relevant changes and right to be excluded from the public extract of the register. In practice, similar information accompanies the copy supplied by English and Welsh authorities. The obligation to supply a copy of the entry also provides authority's with the opportunity to supply chargepayers with information on, and a claim form for, community charge benefit.

The chargepayer's right to inspect his or her register entry

EW reg 10 **9.4** A registered chargepayer has a right to:
S Act s 20

☐ inspect his or her entry in the register;
☐ obtain a copy of the entry.

9.5 Inspection may take place at a reasonable place and time stated by the registration officer. This is usually normal office opening hours. To secure confidentiality no other member of the public may inspect the chargepayer's entry. PN No.6 (para. 5.2) states that where chargepayers want to inspect their register entry they should be required to show some proof of identity before being allowed to do so. It advises that registration officers should consider whether more stringent checks on identity are needed where the entry is for a person whose name does not appear on the public extract (para. 9.14).

S SI 1988 **9.6** Where the register is not kept in written form a reproduction,
No.1539 reg 19 e.g. computer print out, may be supplied. In England and Wales the authority may make a reasonable charge for a copy of the entry. In Scotland the chargepayer may obtain a copy of the entry for £1 or a copy certified by, or on behalf of, the registration officer for £3.

Public right to inspect extracts from the register and lists of designated buildings

EW reg 11 **9.7** The registration officer must compile and maintain:
S Act s 20

☐ an extract from the register of addresses, names and in Scotland the collective charge multiplier for premises subject to the collective charge; and

☐ in England and Wales a list of the buildings designated (para. 5.5) for the collective charge.

9.8 For England and Wales the legislation does not specify a date by which the registration officer must publish the extract. PN No. 6 (para. 2.3) advises that the extract should be published within a reasonable time scale. The extract need not be updated more frequently than every 6 months. In Scotland the extract has been available since 1 April 1989 and the registration officer must update the extract on 1 April and 1 October each year.

EW reg 11   **9.9** In England and Wales the extract must show only an:

☐ address;
☐ surname or family name of the chargepayer;
☐ the initial letter of other names.

9.10 It must not:

☐ be organised by chargepayer name;
☐ show courtesy titles, e.g. Ms, Mr, Mrs, etc;
☐ show the type or amount of community charge the individual is liable to pay; or
☐ show any other information.

S Act s 20   **9.11** In Scotland the extract must show: the address, chargepayer name and the collective charge multiplier for premises subject to the collective charge.

9.12 In England and Wales, anyone may inspect the extract at a reasonable place and time stated by the registration officer. In Scotland the extract may be inspected at the headquarters of the relevant island, regional and district council.

9.13 The extract is made available 'to satisfy public confidence in the accuracy of the register' (PN No. 3, para. 1.7). In other words people can reassure themselves that other individuals are also liable for the charge. The registration officer may not, however, supply a copy of the extract or list to anyone. This overturns the original intention for Scotland at least that the extract should be available for sale to private companies, etc. PN No. 6 (para. 5.2) points out, however, that this prohibition does not stop members of the public making their own copies and they may do so at the registration officer's discretion.

Exclusion from the public extract

EW reg 11
S Act s 20A
S SI 1988
No.1539 reg 18

9.14 The registration officer must omit a name from the public extract if, in his or her opinion, its inclusion might result in anyone (or in Scotland, that person) being subject to a threat of violence. This is known as an anonymous entry in England and Wales, and as a special entry in Scotland. This could apply, e.g., to: people who have left their partners, political refugees, certain government or service personnel and jurors. Individuals liable for the community charge still have to pay it even if their names are excluded from the public extract.

9.15 The reference to 'anyone' in the English and Welsh legislation enables the registration officer to exclude the name of other individuals, e.g. those belonging to the same household such as an adult son or daughter. This is to stop the threatened person being traced through those other individuals.

9.16 The time delay allowed for updating the extract (para. 9.8) allows someone to apply for exclusion between the date of registration and the date their name would be available in the extract. This would be relevant, e.g., where someone else has made a return on the individual's behalf. PN No.6 (para. 2.3) comments that where the extract is made available via a computer screen the registration officer needs to ensure that a suitable time delay exists between someone being registered and their name being accessible through the extract on screen.

9.17 PN No. 6 (paras. 2.5–2.6) advises that there is an opportunity for the registration officer to point out the facility for exclusion in all communication with the chargepayer.

9.18 PN No. 6 suggests that after notification of any new or changed item on the register (para. 8.20) the registration officer should allow 21 days from notification of the register entry for a person to lodge a request to have his or her name excluded from the public extract. In

Scotland a new or amended entry that includes a change of address cannot be included in the public extract within 28 days of the chargepayer being supplied with a copy of the entry. Subsequently, any individual has the right to request the removal of his or her name from the public extract by contacting the office of the registration officer.

APPLICATION FOR EXCLUSION

S Act 20A   **9.19** The applicant should state the reason for exclusions and supply any supporting documents or evidence.

9.20 Where an application is received the registration officer should:

☐ delay inclusion of the individual's details in the public extract;
☐ consider the application and make any necessary further enquiries;
☐ advise the individual of the decision.

THE DECISION TO EXCLUDE SOMEONE FROM THE PUBLIC EXTRACT

9.21 PN No. 6 (para. 4.1) considers that an application should be refused only if:

☐ it is obviously frivolous: or
☐ the applicant can show no relevant reason for wishing to be excluded from the extract.

9.22 The registration officer needs to be reasonably satisfied that an individual's request for exclusion from the public extract is well founded. The registration officer notifies the applicant of the decision. In Scotland this must be done within 2 months of the day the application was received.

9.23 In England and Wales there is no right of appeal against a registration officer's refusal to exclude someone from the public extract. Such a decision could, however, be the subject of judicial review in the High Court. In Scotland, the applicant may appeal to the Sheriff. An appeal may also be made against a registration officer's decision to end the exclusion.

Inspection of the records of a landlord subject to the collective charge

EW Act sch 2
para 18
EW reg 12

9.24 In England and Wales where the authority or registration officer has received a copy of the records of a landlord subject to the collective charge those records must be available for inspection by anyone who is liable to pay a contribution (para. 6.4) to that landlord.

Others who must be provided with information

9.25 In addition to the authority which has access to the register for the setting, billing and collecting of the charge, a number of other public officials have the right to be provided with, or inspect, the register.

OTHER REGISTRATION OFFICERS

S Act s 17
S SI 1989
No.1371

9.26 Throughout Great Britain registration officers must provide other registration officers with information in their possession or control which is reasonably required in connection with community charge registration functions.

EW Act sch 2
para 13

9.27 In England and Wales the registration officer may supply useful information to other registration officers even if not requested to do so and a number of commercial data exchange systems, such as CIPFA's Community Charge Communication Service, have been set up to enable this exchange of information to take place.

THE ASSESSOR, ELECTORAL REGISTRATION OFFICER AND AUDITORS

S Act s 20

9.28 In Scotland the assessor or electoral registration officer may inspect the full register for their area but not those entries excluded from the public extract. In practice the assessor is the electoral registration officer and the registration officer. Presumably therefore the exception must relate to the staff of the different offices rather than the individual office holder.

EW Act s 29   **9.29** In England and Wales the electoral registration officer may inspect any authority's register.

9.30 In Scotland an auditor under section 97(6) of the Local Government (Scotland) Act 1973 may inspect the register whilst auditing the authority's accounts or carrying out other functions under Part VII of that Act.

SECRETARY OF STATE

EW Act s 26A
S Act s 20C

9.31 The registration officer and the authority must supply the Secretary of State with any non-personal information that may be required to enable the Secretary of State to carry out any functions under the Local Government Finance Act 1988 or the Abolition of Domestic Rates Etc (Scotland) Act 1987. Personal information is information which relates to an identifiable living or dead individual. Thus the kind of information that should be asked for or supplied is, e.g., the total number of people who are recorded on the register and the numbers that are exempt.

EW Act ss 27, 28

9.32 Also in England and Wales where the Secretary of State thinks that the register is inadequate, e.g. that the registration officer is failing to register people, then additional information may be requested from the registration officer or the authority. For instance, the Secretary of State may wish to know the number of staff working on registration. The Secretary of State may require that a new canvass be carried out or that additional staff, accommodation or other resources be provided.

KEEPER OF THE RECORDS OF SCOTLAND

S Act s 20
S SI 1988
No.1539 reg 20

9.33 Every Scottish registration officer must supply the Keeper of the Records of Scotland with a copy of the register as soon as practicable after 1 April each year. This is to assist with historical research at a later date. The Keeper may not make the registers or any copies or extracts available to the public for 30 years after the end of the year in which they were supplied.

Other disclosures

9.34 In almost all authorities the register is kept on computer and is therefore, with the exception of the public extract, subject to the requirements of the Data Protection Act 1984. Information held on the register or collected and retained to administer the community charge should not be used or disclosed for purposes other than those authorised or required by statute. An individual who suffers damage or distress as a result of the unauthorised disclosure of his or her data may claim compensation from the registration officer under the Data Protection Act.

EW Act s 13A
S Act s 20C

9.35 Regulations may be made which enable the registration officer to provide non-personal information (para. 9.31) to anyone who requests it for a fee.

CHAPTER 10

Bills and payments

10.1 This chapter explains how personal, standard and collective community charge contributions are billed and collected. It covers:

- ☐ issuing bills;
- ☐ bills for personal, standard and, in Scotland, collective charges: how are they calculated and when must they be paid;
- ☐ bills for collective charges in England and Wales: how are they calculated and when must they be paid; and
- ☐ rules on joint and several liability for couples, managers and others.

10.2 This chapter does not apply to collective contributions (Chapter 6). Chapter 11 explains how authorities may recover unpaid bills.

Issuing bills

WHO RECEIVES A BILL?

EW Act s 7
EW regs 13,14
S Act sch 2

10.3 Bills (also known as 'demand notices') are issued by the authority responsible for collecting the community charge (paras 1.20–23). They are issued to everyone who is shown in the community charge register (Chapter 8) as liable to pay any community charge. If someone is liable for more than one community charge (e.g. a personal and a standard charge) a separate bill is issued for each.

EW Act s 18
EW reg 19

10.4 The chargepayer has a duty to pay any properly issued bill. If he or she fails to do so, the authority may be able to take action for the arrears (Chapter 11). If the amount is wrong, he or she may be able to appeal (paras 12.14–16).

10.5 If more than one person in a household is liable to pay a personal charge, each person receives an individual bill. However, some authorities invite one person to pay the bills of the other household members. The choice is entirely up to the chargepayers concerned. If the arrangement comes unstuck, each chargepayer still has to pay his or her own bill; though if there are arrears, it may then be difficult for the authority to know whose account to show them on. Additional administrative questions are discussed in the practice notes, *Billing for the Community Charge* (PN No. 11, section 7) and *Collection of the Community Charge* (PN No. 12, section 5).

THE CONTENTS OF THE BILL

S Act sch 2
S SI 1988
No.1880

10.6 Bills for the community charge must be in the required format. In Scotland, this is laid down in regulations. In England, the practice note describes the government's plans on this (PN No. 11, para. 2.3 and section 8). Further details are awaited on the format of bills in Wales. However, in each case, the bill must provide information on how it was calculated and when it must be paid. For collective charges in England and Wales, different rules apply. The rules are summarised in paras 10.48–59.

10.7 In England (only) the bill must also compare the actual personal charge set by the authority with the government estimate of the 'amount needed to pay for the standard level of service'. This is designed in part to encourage chargepayers to evaluate the efficiency of the authority in using its funds.

10.8 The calculation of a bill for a personal charge may also take into account adjustments to community charge benefit entitlement. Any bill may also include an amount for a penalty (para. 11.14). The practice note suggests (PN No. 12, para. 2.4) that a bill may also include an amount for arrears from a previous year. However, in England and Wales this can only be the case if no bill has previously been raised for those arrears, since the law provides that arrears which have already been billed continue to be covered by the original bill only. Nonetheless, it is open to the authority to negotiate an appropriate payment pattern for recovering arrears.

WHEN ARE BILLS ISSUED?

EW reg 14
S Act sch 2
S SI 1989
No.2167

10.9 Everyone who is liable for a charge at the beginning of the financial year gets a bill then. In England and Wales these bills must be issued on the day the authority sets its community charge (which must normally be done by 1 April), or as soon as practicable after that. In Scotland they must be issued by 31 March or, if for any reason a bill is omitted, as soon as this comes to light.

EW reg 15
S Act sch 2

10.10 Someone who only becomes liable for a charge later in the year, gets a bill then. The bill must be issued on the day he or she is first liable for the charge, or as soon as practicable after that. The practice note (PN No. 11, para. 5.2) suggests that bills may be issued shortly before that date.

EW reg 14
S Act sch 2

10.11 If someone is liable for the same charge for 2 or more non-consecutive periods, the above rules apply for each such period.

EW reg 15
S Act sch 2

10.12 If liability for a community charge is backdated (para. 8.14) the bill must be issued as soon as possible after the backdated entry is included in the register. In these circumstances in particular, a delay in issuing a bill may result in the charge concerned not being fully recoverable by the authority (para. 11.32).

HOW ARE BILLS ISSUED?

EW reg 2

10.13 Bills may be posted, or delivered in person to the chargepayer or someone else on the premises, or left at or fixed to the chargepayer's address. The date of issue is the date on which it was posted, delivered, left, etc. In the case of a bill which is posted, the chargepayer may be in a position to prove that it never arrived at all (in which case it must be reissued if the authority wishes to use the enforcement procedure). Proving that it arrived late does not change the fact that the date of issue is the date of posting (PN No. 11, paras. 2.4–8).

METHOD OF PAYMENT

10.14 Authorities are free to offer various methods of payment. These may include cash payments, payments by cheque, giro, standing orders, etc. If the authoritiy issues community charge benefit vouchers (para. 7.61), it must accept payment (in part or full) of collective charges by those vouchers. Many authorities are encouraging payment by direct debit in order to keep arrears and transactions to a minimum. People with direct debit arrangements must still be sent bills in the ordinary way.

OVERPAYMENTS

EW reg 50
S Act sch 2

10.15 In any of the circumstances described in this chapter, if the chargepayer has a right to repayment of any community charge, he or she may, if necessary, take court action to recover it from the authority.

Personal, standard and, in Scotland, collective charges

10.16 This section describes the calculation of bills for personal and standard charges in England, Wales and Scotland, and for collective charges in Scotland only. It includes details of the relevant instalment scheme and other rules about when bills are due. Collective charges in Scotland are dealt with separately (paras 10.48 onwards).

THE AMOUNT OF THE BILL

EW reg 16

10.17 If a bill is for a future period, it is estimated up to the end of the financial year (31 March), as described in para. 10.20. This applies:

☐ for all bills issued at the beginning of the financial year (para. 10.9). These bills are therefore for a whole year's community charge; and
☐ when someone becomes liable during the course of the year (para. 10.10). These bills are therefore for the proportion of the year from the date the person becomes liable.

EW regs 16,19

10.18 If a bill is wholly for a past period, and the person is no longer liable for the charge concerned, it is for the actual amount of liability. Separate bills for each financial year must be issued where applicable.

EW reg 16

10.19 If a bill includes a past period, and the person is still liable for the charge concerned, it is for the actual amount of liability for the past period, and is estimated up to the end of the financial year, as described in para. 10.20. This would apply, e.g., where a bill included a backdated amount (para. 10.12).

ASSUMPTIONS MADE IN ESTIMATING BILLS

EW regs 13,16   **10.20** Bills for future periods are estimated, with any subsequent change in the chargepayer's circumstances taken into account when they occur (paras 10.28, 10.38). In Scotland, it is up to the authority how to make an estimate for a future period. In England and Wales the authority must make the estimate on the assumption that the chargepayer's circumstances (as shown on the register on the day the bill is issued) will not change during the remainder of the financial year. In particular, that:

☐   the person will remain subject to the charge (e.g. will not move, or will not become exempt);

☐   a student in full-time advanced education (in the case of a personal charge) will remain in full-time advanced education;

☐   any community charge benefit to which the person is entitled (in the case of a personal charge) will not change.

10.21 The last assumption only applies if the chargepayer has been notified of the amount. The practice note recommends that wherever possible bills should be net of any entitlement to community charge benefit (PN No. 11, para. 2.12). It is obviously equally desirable for bills for personal charges to be net of entitlement to transitional relief (Chapter 7). It is up to the authority whether to make any assumptions not listed above.

WHEN MUST THE BILL BE PAID?

10.22 Bills may be paid under the statutory instalment scheme or an alternative payment pattern. The remainder of this section deals with each of these in turn, followed by general rules applying in both cases.

WHICH BILLS MAY BE PAID UNDER THE STATUTORY INSTALMENT SCHEME?

EW reg 17
S Act sch 2   **10.23** Payment under the statutory instalment scheme is available as of right to all personal and standard chargepayers and also, in Scotland, to collective chargepayers – though there are certain exceptions (para. 10.24). The English and Welsh version of the scheme differs from that in Scotland, and the 2 are described in detail below. In general, the effect of the scheme is that charges

due for the whole year may be paid in 10 instalments in England and Wales, and in 12 instalments in Scotland (though see para. 10.41). The bill (or an accompanying notice) must require payments to be made by this method, unless the authority and the chargepayer have agreed an alternative payment pattern (para. 10.40).

EW reg 17
S Act sch 2

10.24 The statutory instalment scheme does not apply:

☐ for bills issued by housing bodies in Scotland unless the agency arrangement they have with with the regional council (para. 1.22) requires them to apply it. When it does not apply, it is up to the authority to decide on an alternative payment pattern;

☐ in Scotland, for any amount relating to a period before the bill is issued (whether the whole bill or any part of it). Such an amount is due in full in the month following the date of issue, on whatever day in that month the authority chooses;

☐ in England and Wales, if the whole amount of the bill relates to a period before the bill is issued. The authority must require payment within a specified period, which must not be less than 14 days after the date of issue.

THE STATUTORY INSTALMENT SCHEME IN ENGLAND AND WALES: GENERAL RULES

EW regs sch 1

10.25 In England and Wales, the statutory instalment scheme applies for the personal and standard community charge. The number of instalments in the scheme depends on when the bill is issued (Table 10.1). When there are 2 or more instalments, these must be due in consecutive months. The authority chooses which months and which day of the month, and these can vary from chargepayer to chargepayer. When there is one instalment, the authority chooses which day it is to be due. In each case, the first (or only) instalment must not fall due until at least 14 days after the bill.

Table 10.1

STATUTORY INSTALMENT SCHEME: ENGLAND AND WALES

Month in which the bill is issued	Number of instalments
April (or before)	10
May	9
June	8
July	7
August	6
September	5
October	4
November	3
December	2
January (or after)	1

10.26 The amount of each instalment is calculated as follows:

☐ if there are 2 or more instalments, each instalment must be of equal amount, rounded to the nearest multiple of 10p, with any adjustment being made in the first instalment only;

☐ if any resulting instalment would be less than £5, the number of instalments is reduced until each instalment is at least £5. The authority chooses which months they are to be in, but they must be consecutive, and the first instalment must not fall due until at least 14 days after the issue of the bill;

☐ if the total amount due is less than £10, there is a single instalment only. The authority chooses when it is to be due, but it must not be until at least 14 days after the issue of the bill.

Examples
ENGLAND AND WALES

Total amount due £400. Bill issued on 1 April.

10 instalments of £40 are due. The earliest instalment can be on 15 April. These can be in any 10 consecutive months (i.e. April to January, May to February or June to March).

Total amount due £234.56. Bill issued on 19 April.

9 instalments of £23.50 are due, preceded by one instalment of £23.06. The earliest instalment can be on 3 May. The instalments can be in any 10 consecutive months excluding April (i.e. May to February or June to March).

Total amount due £91. Bill issued on 1 July.

7 instalments of £13 are due. The earliest instalment can be on 15 July. The instalments can be in any 7 consecutive months from July onwards (July to March or August to April).

Total amount due £50. Bill issued on 1 January.

One instalment of £50 is due. The earliest due date can be on 15 January. Any alternative date may be chosen after that.

Total amount due £18. Bill issued on 1 April.

Dividing £18 by 10 results in less than £5. 3 instalments are therefore due, of £6 each. The earliest can be on 15 April. The instalments can be in any 3 consecutive months (e.g. April to June, August to October, January to March).

Total amount due £7. Bill issued on 1 April.

This is less than £10, so there can only be one instalment. The earliest due date can be on 15 April. Any alternative date may be chosen after that.

THE STATUTORY INSTALMENT SCHEME IN ENGLAND AND WALES: END OF LIABILITY FOR A CHARGE

10.27 This paragraph describes what happens in the statutory instalment scheme when liability for a personal or standard community charge ends. In all events no further instalments are due. The authority must send a notice to the chargepayer stating his or her revised liability for the financial year (i.e. up to the last day of liability). This is compared with the amount of instalments already due (whether or not paid):

☐ if the revised liability is greater, the authority must require the chargepayer to pay the balance within a specified period, which must not be less than 14 days after the issue of the notice;

☐ if the revised liability is lower, the balance is first put towards any arrears which have accrued. After that, if there remains an overpayment, the authority must repay it to the chargepayer if he or she requires this. Otherwise, the authority may choose to repay it, or choose to credit it against any future liability he or she may have.

Example

ENGLAND AND WALES

A bill for a personal charge of £400 is issued on 1 April requiring 10 instalments of £40 on 23 May to 23 February. The chargepayer then leaves the area on 1 July.

Revised estimate. This is calculated by dividing the annual charge by the number of days in the year and multiplying by the number of days of liability (1 April to 30 June): £400 ÷ 365 × 91 = £99.73.

Instalments already due. 2 instalments have fallen due (on 23 February and 23 March), totalling £80.

Outcome. The authority requires payment of the balance of £19.73. (If the person was in any case in arrears with the instalments already due, this money also remains due under those old instalments).

THE STATUTORY INSTALMENT SCHEME IN ENGLAND AND WALES: OTHER CHANGES IN LIABILITY

10.28 The next paragraph describes what happens in the statutory instalment scheme when the chargepayer's liability changes from that initially foreseen because:

☐ the chargepayer becomes or ceases to be a full-time student in advanced education;

☐ the authority is required to set a substituted personal charge (para. 13.38);

☐ the property changes from one standard community charge class to another and there is a resultant change in the multiplier;

☐ the chargepayer becomes entitled to community charge benefit, or his or her entitlement changes; or

☐ there has been an overpayment of community charge benefit and the authority has decided to add this to the chargepayer's liability (para. 7.62).

10.29 The authority must send a notice to the chargepayer stating its revised estimate of his or her liability for the year (i.e. assuming there will be no further changes). This is compared with the amount of instalments at the old rate which are already due or which will be due up to 14 days after the date of issue of the notice (whether or not paid):

☐ if the revised estimate is greater, the balance is then divided amongst the instalment dates due 14 days or more after the notice. (This 'new' rate is calculated according to the general rules about instalments. The authority cannot create new instalment dates.) If there are no such instalment dates, the authority must require the balance to be paid within a specified period, which must not be less than 14 days;

☐ if the revised estimate is lower, the balance is first put towards any arrears which have accrued. After that, if there remains an overpayment, the authority must repay it to the chargepayer if he or she requires this. Otherwise, the authority may choose to repay it, or choose to credit it against any future liability he or she may have.

10.30 If there is a further change, the process is repeated, except that any amounts already repaid (or already credited to the chargepayer's account) are treated as never having been due.

Examples

ENGLAND AND WALES

An authority's personal community charge is £365. A student chargepayer in the area receives a bill for £73, due in 10 instalments of £7.30 on 23 May to 23 February. However, he ceases to be a registered student on 30 June. The authority issues its notice about this on 20 July.

Revised estimate. This is calculated as:

91 days (1 April to 30 June) at £0.20 per day	£ 18.20
274 days (1 July to 31 March) at £1.00 per day	£274.00
Total	£292.20

Instalments at the old rate. 2 instalments have fallen due (in May and June), and the July instalment is less than 14 days after the revised notice. There are 3 instalments at the old rate, totalling £21.90.

Outcome. A balance remains due for the year of:

Revised estimate	£292.20
Less instalments due at the old rate	£ 21.90
Balance	£270.30

This is recovered from the 7 instalments due on 23 August to 23 February. The first instalment is £38.70; the remainder, £38.60.

The chargepayer in the above example takes up a fresh course and becomes a student again from 1 October. The council issues its notice on 4 October.

Revised estimate. This is now in 3 parts:

91 days (1 April to 30 June) at £0.20 per day	£ 18.20
92 days (1 July to 30 Sept) at £1.00 per day	£ 92.00
182 days (1 Oct to 31 March) at £0.20 per day	£ 36.40
Total	£146.60

Instalments at the old rates. 3 instalments have fallen due at £7.30 (in May, June and July). 2 instalments have fallen due (August and September) at £38.70 and £38.60 respectively. So the total of instalments at the old rates is £99.20.

Examples, continued

Outcome. A balance remains due for the year of:

Revised estimate	£146.60
Less instalments due at the old rate	£ 99.20
Balance	£ 47.40

This is recovered from the 5 instalments due on 23 October to 23 February. The first instalment is £9.40; the remainder, £9.50.

THE STATUTORY INSTALMENT SCHEME IN ENGLAND
AND WALES: FAILURE TO PAY INSTALMENTS

EW reg 20   **10.31** If the chargepayer fails to pay any instalment, the authority must issue a reminder detailing the outstanding amounts. Seven days after it is issued, if there are outstanding arrears of any instalments due by then, the chargepayer loses the right to pay by instalments. Instead, he or she is liable for the remaining, most recent estimated amount for the whole financial year, and this is due 14 days after the issue of the reminder. Authorities are unlikely to insist upon such a tight time scale, however, preferring instead to issue further reminders and to allow longer periods for payment of the arrears.

10.32 The authority may revise an estimate if any of the factors taken into account are shown to be incorrect, and must do so if the chargepayer requires it. The authority must notify the chargepayer of the revised estimate. If the recalculated amount is higher, the authority may require the chargepayer to make an interim payment of the difference, due within a specified period which must not be less than 14 days. If the recalculated amount is lower, the authority may make an interim repayment to the chargepayer. Alternatively, it may credit it towards the chargepayer's future liability, but only in cases where liability for one community charge ends during a financial year and is then immediately followed by liability for another community charge (e.g. where someone moves house within the area).

10.33 Once the actual amount due from the chargepayer is known (at the end of the year, or when the chargepayer ceases to be liable for the charge), there is a final reckoning up. The chargepayer is notified of any balance due, and this remains payable. If any balance is due to the chargepayer, the authority may credit it towards the chargepayer's future liability, but only in cases where liability for one community charge ends during a financial year and is then immediately followed by liability for another community charge. Otherwise the authority must, if the chargepayer requires it, repay it. In all other cases, the authority may choose to repay it or to credit it against any future liability he or she may have.

THE STATUTORY INSTALMENT SCHEME IN SCOTLAND: GENERAL RULES

S Act sch 2
S SI 1988
No.1880

10.34 In Scotland, the statutory instalment scheme applies for personal, standard and collective charges, and also for the community water charge collected with them.

10.35 For all bills issued before the beginning of the financial year to which they apply (i.e. before 1 April), payment is due in 12 equal monthly instalments on whatever day in each month the authority chooses. This may (except in the first month) be rounded to the nearest 5p.

10.36 For bills issued between 1 April and 31 December inclusive, payment is due by monthly instalments. In the case of personal and standard charges, this is calculated at one twelfth of the annual equivalent for whole months, with the balance due in the first month. For bills issued on or after 1 January, the whole amount of the bill is due on whatever day the authority chooses.

10.37 If, in any case where there are instalments, the total amount due is less than £24, or any instalment is less than £2 (in each case net of any community charge benefit), the authority may either choose to bill the whole amount in the month following the date of issue of the bill, on whatever day it chooses; or choose to bill the amount by monthly instalments on whatever days of whatever months it chooses, so long as none of the instalments is less than £2.

10.38 There are no separate rules for recalculating instalments in the event of a change of circumstances. The above apply with appropriate variations.

THE STATUTORY INSTALMENT SCHEME IN SCOTLAND: FAILURE TO PAY INSTALMENTS

S Act s 21   **10.39** If the chargepayer fails to pay any 3 instalments (whether consecutive or not), he or she loses the right to pay by instalments. Instead the whole remaining amount for the financial year falls due. However, this only applies if the authority notifies the chargepayer accordingly.

ALTERNATIVE PAYMENT PATTERNS

EW reg 17   **10.40** For personal and standard charges and also in Scotland, collective
S Act sch 2   charges, the chargepayer and the authority can agree an alternative payment pattern. This agreement may be made at any time (even if a bill has already been issued under the statutory instalment scheme), and can cover any aspect of payment including those provided for in the statutory instalment scheme. A bill issued after such an agreement must require payment under the alternative payment pattern adopted.

10.41 There are a number of examples of alternative payment patterns. There is nothing to stop a chargepayer paying the whole amount at once at the beginning of the year, and many authorities also offer payment by 2 half-yearly instalments. In Scotland many chargepayers have been invited to pay by 48 instalments using a book of vouchers. In England and Wales, some authorities have offered their council tenants the option of paying community charge at the same time as the rent (e.g. weekly or fortnightly). In such cases, the accounting system must clearly distinguish between payments of rent and community charge. Authorities may also agree an alternative payment pattern when a chargepayer is in arrears, rather than take recovery action.

10.42 In any alternative payment pattern, it is useful for the authority to ensure that provision is made for adjustments in liability. Also, whereas under the statutory instalment scheme there are specific rules for dealing with failure to pay instalments (paras 10.31, 10.39), these do not apply in alternative payment arrangements unless such a provision is specifically included.

DISCOUNT SCHEMES

S Act sch 2   **10.43** In Scotland, the authority may offer a discount if the
S SI 1988   chargepayer enters into an agreement to pay which is financially
No.1880   advantageous to it. The maximum discount is 5 per cent of the bill otherwise due. Generally speaking, authorities only offer such

discounts in cases where payment is made in full at the beginning of the financial year, though other discount schemes are possible. Authorities may offer inducements instead of (or as well as) a discount. These may be financial or of some other nature, including the offer of lottery tickets. The authority may not offer discounts or inducements, or a combination of these, which exceed in financial terms the value to it of the payment arrangements involved.

EW regs 21A, 21B

10.44 In England and Wales, the authority may offer a discount for payments made in full before the date when the first instalment would otherwise have fallen due, so long as at least two instalments would be due under the statutory scheme or an alternative payment pattern. Discounts may also be offered for instalments paid by direct debit, standing order or some other non-cash method. Discount schemes must be decided on before the personal community charge for the year is set, and must apply equally to chargepayers in equivalent circumstances. There is no 5 per cent limit.

CHANGES IN LIABILITY

EW reg 16
S Act sch 2

10.45 Changes in liability are taken into account as and when they occur. In Scotland, a replacement bill is issued in any appropriate case. This is calculated on the new circumstances and supersedes the original bill. In England and Wales, a replacement bill must be issued when the authority is obliged by the Secretary of State to change its personal charge (para. 13.38) or when the standard charge multiplier for a property changes after the issue of a bill. Otherwise, changes of circumstances are catered for by adjustments to the statutory instalment scheme, or under any alternative payment pattern which may have been adopted, or under the rule described in the next paragraphs.

FINAL ADJUSTMENTS

EW reg 26

10.46 This further rule applies in England and Wales if the statutory instalment scheme (or alternative payment pattern if one has been adopted) makes no provision for dealing with outstanding amounts which have not yet been billed, or for dealing with any overpayment. In either case the authority must issue a notice specifying the total amount already billed for the period and the total amount actually due for the period.

EW reg 26

10.47 If the amount actually due is greater than the amount already billed, the authority must issue a final bill for the difference, and require payment within a specified period, which must not be less than 14 days after the date of issue. If the chargepayer has in fact paid more than the amount actually due, the authority must, if the chargepayer requires it, repay the difference. Otherwise the authority may choose to repay it or to credit it against any subsequent liability the chargepayer may have.

Collective charges in England and Wales

10.48 This section describes the calculation of bills for collective charges in England and Wales. It includes details of the relevant instalment scheme and other rules about when bills are due. Collective charges in Scotland are dealt with above (paras 10.16–47).

PAYMENT BY INSTALMENTS

EW regs 18,19 sch 2

10.49 In England and Wales, the demand notice sent to a collective chargepayer at the beginning of the year is not a bill for a specific amount. It cannot be, because the amount depends on the actual numbers of occupiers in the accommodation throughout the year. Instead, it must specify the amount of the personal charge applicable in the area, and require the collective chargepayer to submit returns and make payments. The chargepayer must then fulfil these duties as described below.

EW regs sch 2

10.50 Every calendar month of the year is a 'return period' for collective community chargepayers. The exceptions to this rule are:

☐ in the case of a demand notice issued on or after 1 May for the relevant financial year, the first return period includes the whole of the year up to the end of the preceding month; and

☐ in the case of a demand notice issued after the end of the relevant financial year, the return period is the whole of that year.

EW regs sch 2

10.51 The return must be submitted within 14 days of the end of the return period, or within 14 days of the date of service of the demand notice if later. The return constitutes a schedule of every contribution which has fallen due during the return period, whether or not the chargepayer is able to recover it from his or her residents (para. 5.22), and whether or not they have actually paid. On submission of the return the chargepayer must also submit the total value of all contributions described in the schedule, less a handling fee of 5 per cent (unless an alternative payment pattern has been agreed: para. 10.58).

EW Act sch 3   **10.52** If the chargepayer knowingly submits a return which is materially inaccurate (i.e. would affect the amount of community charge due), he or she may incur a penalty (Chapter 11), or could be prosecuted under the Theft Act.

LOSS OF RIGHT TO PAY BY INSTALMENTS

EW reg 21   **10.53** A further rule applies if the chargepayer fails to meet the obligation to submit a return or make a payment within 14 days of when it is due. He or she loses the right to pay by instalments, and is instead liable for the remaining estimated amount for the whole financial year. If the authority issues a bill stating the estimated amount and requiring payment, the amount becomes payable 7 days after the issue of the bill. Authorities are unlikely to insist upon such a tight time scale, preferring instead to issue a reminder and allow chargepayer more time to fulfil their duties.

EW reg 21   **10.54** The estimate is made by the authority on the assumptions that:

- ☐ if the chargepayer is liable for the collective charge on the date of issue of the notice, he or she will remain liable for the remainder of the year;
- ☐ if the chargepayer is not liable for the collective charge on the date of issue of the notice, he or she will not be liable again during the remainder of the year.

EW reg 21   **10.55** To assist in the making of this estimate, the authority may write requesting the chargepayer to supply any specified information within 21 days. The chargepayer need only supply information in his or her possession or control. Failure do to so may incur a penalty (Chapter 11).

EW reg 21   **10.56** The authority may choose to revise an estimate which it believes to be inaccurate (and para. 10.32 also applies here). Also, if the chargepayer makes all the returns for a period (not necessarily a whole financial year), he or she may require the authority to make a revised estimate taking them into account. In either case, if the recalculated amount is higher, the authority may require the chargepayer to make an interim payment of the difference. If the recalculated amount is lower, the authority may make an interim repayment to the chargepayer.

EW reg 21   **10.57** Once the actual amount due from the chargepayer is known (e.g. at the end of the financial year, or if he or she ceases to be liable for a charge), there is a final reckoning up. A bill is issued for any balance due from the chargepayer, requiring payment within a specified period, which must not be less than 14 days after the date of issue. If any balance is due to the chargepayer, the authority must, if he or she requires it, repay it. Otherwise the authority may choose to repay it or to credit against any subsequent liability he or she may have.

ALTERNATIVE PAYMENT PATTERNS

EW regs sch 2   **10.58** Whilst the pattern of return periods described above (para. 10.50) may not be varied, it is possible for the chargepayer and the authority to agree an alternative payment pattern. Neither authority nor chargepayer can impose an alternative pattern on each other. But by mutual agreement, they could arrange that payments were to be quarterly; or that, though paid monthly, they were to be of the same amount each month, with a final reckoning up at the end of the year. In such cases, an agreement can be made at any time, whether before or after a demand notice has been issued.

DISCOUNTS AND FINAL ADJUSTMENTS

10.59 It is unlikely that a discount scheme will apply for collective charges in England and Wales. The rules on final adjustments, described in paras 10.46–47 also apply for collective charges in England and Wales.

Joint and several liability

10.60 The next few paragraphs describe the additional rules relating to joint and several liability for:

☐ couples;
☐ landlords and managers; and
☐ co-owners.

MARRIED AND UNMARRIED COUPLES

EW Act s 16
EW reg 22
S Act s 8

10.61 Couples may have to pay one another's community charges. This only applies for couples of opposite sex who live together and are married or living together as husband and wife; and only for personal charges and, in England and Wales, for standard charges. The rule does not apply in England and Wales to partners under 18, but does apply in Scotland in such cases. It does apply throughout Great Britain to partners who are registered students or who are exempt from a personal community charge.

10.62 Couples may also be jointly and severally liable under different rules, usually relating to co-owners: paras 10.79–80. This might apply for collective charges and, in Scotland, for standard charges. There are no rules which could make couples jointly and severally liable for collective contributions.

10.63 The rule only applies for any period where the partners are members of the same household/living together. For example, if they fulfil this condition for only part of a financial year, the rule can only be invoked for that part of the year, and for the appropriately apportioned part of the bill in question (as described below). In particular, in England and Wales, this is defined as excluding the day during which the couple begin or cease to fulfil the condition.

EW reg 23
S Act sch 2

10.64 However, no partner is liable to make a payment under this rule unless the authority issues a bill to him or her. In Scotland, authorities are specifically prohibited from doing this until such time as it appears they will be unable to recover the charge from the chargepayer: any bill follows the ordinary rules on bills. In England and Wales, the following rules apply. Authorities may not bill a partner until the chargepayer has failed to pay an amount due, other than simply a penalty (e.g. it is not possible to do so when a bill is first issued at the beginning of the year). Furthermore, in the case of a missed instalment under the statutory instalment scheme, a reminder must have been sent and 7 days must have passed without payment being made. A bill to a partner must request the whole outstanding amount within a specified period, which must not be less than 14 days: rules about the amount of the bill (including an adjusted bill) are described below (paras 10.75–78).

EW Act s 16

10.65 When this rule is used in England and Wales, the partner who does the paying may recover the money from the partner whose charge it was, if the latter failed to pay it 'because of wilful refusal or culpable neglect'; and may if necessary take court action to do so. In all other cases, it is left to the couple to settle the matter between them.

WHEN MAY JOINT AND SEVERAL LIABILITY FOR COUPLES BE USED?

10.66 The practice note, *Joint and Several Liability*, strongly recommends that authorities should not automatically invoke joint and several liability (PN No. 16, para. 3.3). It points out (PN No. 16, para. 2.3) that a married couple may be jointly and severally liable even if they are registered for personal charges at separate addresses. This is because the definition of a couple for the purposes of joint and several liability does not depend on the notion of 'sole or main residence', but in England and Wales refers to married couples 'who are members of the same household', a phrase taken directly from social security legislation; and in Scotland, to married couples who 'live together'.

10.67 The definition does not include the extension (in much social security legislation) to polygamous marriages. In effect this leaves open the question of whether any 2 partners of a polygamous marriage might constitute a couple, though the practice note recommends that they do (PN No. 16, para. 2.9). In theory it also leaves open the question of which permutation(s) of 2 partners in an unmarried polygamous relationship might constitute a couple.

10.68 On the other hand it is clear that, when a couple separate or divorce, joint and several liability ceases for any future period. There remains the option of invoking joint and several liability for the period when they lived together. The practice note (PN No. 16, section 4) gives examples of when this might be appropriate. There are also various examples of when it would not be appropriate. For instance, if a woman has fled the home because of violence, with no access to financial help from her former partner, it would seem wholly wrong to insist she pay any arrears he may have left behind. In such a case, the authority should be willing to wait until it is able to enforce the arrears against the man. The matter remains largely at the discretion of authorities, who are therefore encouraged to formulate adequate policies so that staff are aware of what is and is not reasonable.

10.69 It should be emphasised that joint and several liability does not arise in any other relationship. So no-one can be obliged to pay the community charge of an adult son or daughter (or other relative) who lives with him or her (or elsewhere). The authority must therefore take care not to assume automatically that 2 people of opposite sex at the same address are necessarily a couple. They cannot in fact insist on this information until after a liability order has been obtained from the magistrates' court (para. 11.41), at which stage it may be possible for the chargepayer to appeal on the grounds that joint and several liability does not apply.

MANAGEMENT ARRANGEMENTS

EW Act s 17
EW reg 22

10.70 In England and Wales only, joint and several liability may also arise for standard and collective charges where a property is managed by someone else on behalf of the chargepayer. For example, this can apply when a collective community charge hostel is owned by a housing association but the rent is collected by a voluntary housing group. In such cases the manager can be called on to pay the standard or collective community charge bill for whatever period the conditions are fulfilled. If the conditions are fulfilled for only part of a financial year, the rule can only be invoked for that part of the year, and for the appropriately apportioned part of the bill in question. In particular, it does apply for the day on which the agreement begins and for the day on which it ends.

EW Act s 17

10.71 For standard charges, the rule applies only if the following conditions are satisfied throughout the period in question:

☐ the chargepayer has an arrangement with a manager to collect rent or contributions or other payments on the property;
☐ the chargepayer is a company (not an individual);
☐ the manager may be either a company or an individual. In the latter case he or she must not be the chargepayer's employee and must be aged at least 18.

EW Act s 17

10.72 For collective charges, the rule applies only if the following conditions are satisfied throughout the period in question:

☐ the chargepayer has an arrangement with a manager to collect rent or other payments on the property;
☐ the chargepayer may be either a company or an individual;

☐ the manager may be either a company or an individual. In the latter case he or she must not be the chargepayer's employee and must be aged at least 18.

EW reg 23   **10.73** However, no manager has to make a payment under this rule unless the authority issues a bill; and the authority may not do so until the chargepayer has failed to pay an amount due, other than simply a penalty (as in para. 10.64). A bill sent to a manager must request the whole outstanding amount within a specified period, which must not be less than 14 days: rules about the amount of the bill (including an adjusted bill) are described below (paras 10.75–78).

EW Act s 17   **10.74** When this rule is used, the manager has the right to recover any payment made to the authority from the chargepayer, and may if necessary take court action to do so.

JOINT AND SEVERAL LIABILITY FOR COUPLES AND MANAGERS: THE AMOUNT OF THE BILL

EW Act ss 16,17   **10.75** When joint and several liability for couples or managers is
EW regs 22,23   invoked, the amount of the bill is calculated according to specific rules. These apply in England and Wales only. However, similar principles are likely to be adopted in Scotland. The rules refer in particular to a 'chargeable period' which is:

☐ the whole of the period for which the person was actually liable for the charge in question, from the beginning of the financial year up to the date of issue of the bill; plus

☐ where the charge in question is a standard community charge, and for part of the financial year to date the standard community charge multiplier has been 0, any such period; plus

☐ where the bill is issued before the end of the period in question, the whole of the remainder of the financial year.

EW reg 23   **10.76** If the bill is issued at or after the end of the chargeable period, the amount is calculated as follows:

☐ the amount of charge due for the whole of the chargeable period during which joint and several liability actually existed, up to and including the date of issue of the bill;

☐ minus any payment already received for that period. If the chargeable period included any days during which joint and several liability did not exist, any payment the person has actually made is assumed to apply first to those days; and if a penalty was included in the original bill, any payment already made is assumed to apply to it first.

EW reg 23   **10.77** If the bill is issued before the end of the chargeable period, the amount for the period up to and including the date of issue of the bill is calculated as in the preceding paragraph. The amount for the remaining future period is calculated on the assumptions that:

☐ the chargepayer will remain subject to the charge throughout the year;
☐ if joint and several liability has actually existed throughout the chargeable period up to and including the date of issue of the bill, it will continue to do so throughout the remainder of the chargeable period;
☐ if joint and several liability has actually existed for only a proportion of the chargeable period up to and including the date of issue of the bill, it will continue to exist for the same proportion of the remainder of the chargeable period;
☐ any other relevant circumstances of the case will remain as they are at the date of issue of the bill.

EW reg 23   **10.78** Should any of the above assumptions turn out to be false, the authority must serve a revised notice on the partner, calculated as above. Should any revised notice be served on the chargeable person as a result of any of the rules on adjustments of bills, an appropriately revised notice must also be served on the partner. In either case, if this results in an increased amount due from the partner, the authority must issue a further bill as described above (paras 10.28–30); if however there has been an overpayment by the partner, the authority must repay the overpayment to the partner if he or she so requires; otherwise it may repay it or credit it to his or her future liability. If the sum concerned exceeds the amount that the partner has paid (excluding any amount he or she has recovered from the chargepayer), any balance must be repaid to the chargepayer if he or she so requires; otherwise it may be repaid or credited as the authority chooses.

Examples

ENGLAND AND WALES

A woman receives a bill for £365 for her personal community charge for the year beginning 1 April 1990, due in 10 instalments of £36.50 on 16th of each month from April to January. On 31 May 1990 a man moves in with her as her unmarried partner. The following are 2 alternative illustrations of this example.

In this illustration, the woman fails to pay any instalments. In June, following an unsuccessful reminder, the authority decides to bill the man for her charge, and to issue the bill to him on 1 August 1990.

Authority action. From 1 April to 31 July, the woman has been liable for 122 days of personal charge. They have been jointly and severally liable from 1 June (because 31 May, the day the man moved in, does not count) to 31 July: 61 days. The bill to the man must therefore be for $^{61}/_{122}$ (= $^{1}/_{2}$) of the total annual amount, which is £182.50. The bill must require payment within 14 days of the date of issue of the bill (or such longer period as the authority decides on).

In this illustration, the woman pays 7 instalments and then stops. Following an unsuccessful reminder, the authority decides to bill the man for her charge, and to issue the bill to him in April 1991.

Authority action. During the whole 1990-91 financial year, they have been jointly and severally liable from 1 June to 31 March: 304 days. The bill must therefore be for $^{304}/_{365}$ of the annual charge of £365 (= £304.00) less the 7 instalments of £36.50 already paid (£255.50) which equals £48.50. The man cannot be billed for the £61 for the period when he did not live there.

Subsequent development. The man in fact pays nothing, but the authority subsequently receives, at intervals, 2 cheques from the woman for £36.50 (explained by her as being late instalments).

Examples, continued

Authority action. The first cheque must be treated as (partly) discharging the woman's liability of £61.00 for the period when the man did not live with her, leaving a balance of (£61.00 – £36.50) = £24.50 due only from her. None of it therefore discharges the man's liability, which remains at £48.50.

The second cheque must first be treated as discharging the balance of £24.50 of the woman's liability for the period when the man did not live with her. The balance of £12.00 must be treated as (partly) discharging the bill sent to the man, leaving him liable for (£48.50 – £12.00) = £36.50. The council may pursue either of them for this remaining amount.

CO-OWNERS

EW Act s 19
EW regs 13,59
60
EW SI 1989
No.1057
S Act ss 10,11

10.79 Further rules, described below, apply in relation to people who jointly own properties which give rise to liability for a standard or collective charge or have a joint tenancy of such properties. The same rules apply if the joint owners or tenants are couples (unless the ordinary rules on joint and several liability for couples apply: para. 10.61). For convenience, these are all referred to as 'co-owners' below. Co-owners are jointly and severally liable for the community charge concerned. That is, any of them can be billed for the whole amount, or an arrangement can be entered into for each to pay part (whether with the authority or informally).

EW reg 59

10.80 In England and Wales, the following further rules apply. If a property is co-owned for only part of a year, separate charges are due for the period of the co-ownership and for the period when the property is not co-owned, in each case calculated on a daily basis for the relevant periods. If the identity of the co-owners of a property changes during the year, then a separate charge is due from each group of co-owners for the relevant periods, calculated on a daily basis. For example, if a property subject to a standard charge is owned solely for the first part of the year, then owned jointly by 3 co-owners for the second part of the year, and then one of the 3 dies leaving 2 co-owners for the remainder of the year; 3 separate community charge bills are issued for the 3 periods (instead of one bill for the whole year). Furthermore, the ordinary rules on joint and several liability for couples and managers described above may be invoked in relation to any of the co-owners concerned.

Death

EW Act s 25
EW reg 61

10.81 Further rules apply on the death of someone who is (or is alleged to have been) liable for any community charge, including cases of joint and several liability of couples or managers. In such cases the executor or administrator of the estate is liable to pay any outstanding amounts from the dead person's estate. If the amount had not yet become payable before the death (perhaps because it was due to be paid by an instalment due after the death) it is only due if the authority serves a notice on the executor or administrator specifying how much it is. If the administrator or executor fails to pay, the authority must pursue this using the ordinary rules in relation to debts of deceased persons, rather than by applying for a liability order in the magistrates' court under community charge provisions. If there was an overpayment of community charge by the dead person, the administrator or executor is entitled to repayment of that sum.

CHAPTER 11

Penalties and enforcement

11.1 This chapter considers:

☐ the penalties relating to the community charge;
☐ the interest and surcharge payable on certain arrears in Scotland; and
☐ enforcement of the community charge.

11.2 Penalties refers to civil penalties imposed for failure to provide information or for the provision of false information for registration or, in England or Wales, collection of community charge. Interest and a surcharge are payable in Scotland on certain arrears of community charge where the chargepayer fails to notify the registration officer of initial liability or a change that would effect the register entry. Enforcement refers to the powers authorities have to recover community charge arrears.

Penalties in England and Wales

DISCRETIONARY NATURE

EW Act s 22
sch 3

11.3 In England and Wales the authority's and the registration officer's powers to impose penalties are discretionary. The Act does not require the imposition of penalties. PN No. 20 (para. 2.1) advises that they should be used with care. An appeal may be made against the imposition of a penalty.

THE AUTHORITY'S POWER TO IMPOSE PENALTIES

EW Act sch 3
para 1

11.4 The authority may impose a £50 penalty on any person it has requested to supply information under any regulation if that person:

☐ fails without reasonable excuse to supply the information; or
☐ knowingly supplies information which is materially inaccurate.

11.5 The term person includes companies but not the registration officer's own authority or another authority.

THE REGISTRATION OFFICER'S POWERS TO IMPOSE PENALTIES

EW Act sch 3
para 2

11.6 The registration officer has exactly the same powers in relation to the compilation and retention of records. A £50 penalty may be imposed where a person:

☐ fails without reasonable excuse to compile or retain records in accordance with regulations; or
☐ knowingly compiles a record which is inaccurate in a material particular.

REPEATED BREACH OF DUTY

EW Act sch 3
paras 1,2

11.7 The authority or registration officer may impose a £200 penalty each time that person:

☐ repeats exactly the same breach of duty; and
☐ a £50 penalty has already been imposed.

SEPARATE POWERS

11.8 The powers to impose penalties by the authority and the registration officer are quite separate. Usually a breach of duty relates to the separate functions of the registration officer, e.g. an individual's failure to complete a canvass return, or the authority, e.g. an individual's failure to supply information for billing purposes.

11.9 Some breaches of duty giving rise to civil penalties relate to both the authority's and the registration officer's functions, e.g. a landlord's failure to supply copies of collective charge records. In such instances a penalty may be imposed by which ever asked for the copies. Certain types of breaches, such as the duty to compile and retain collective charge records (para. 5.33), are relevant to the functions of both the authority and the registration officer. To ensure that the landlord in such a case does not face 2 penalties for the same breach of duty only the registration officer may impose a penalty in such instances.

11.10 A penalty imposed by the authority is invalid if it should have been imposed by the registration officer and vice versa.

POWER TO QUASH A PENALTY

EW Act sch 3
paras 1,2
EW reg 24

11.11 The authority and registration officer have the power to quash a penalty that they have imposed. Where (part of) the penalty has already been paid it may be repaid to the individual concerned by deduction from community charge or another penalty.

CIVIL PENALTIES AND CRIMINAL ACTIVITY

EW Act sch 3
para 3

11.12 A penalty cannot be imposed where a person has been convicted of an offence for the same conduct that gives rise to the penalty.

COLLECTION OF PENALTIES

EW reg 24

11.13 The following relate to penalties that are imposed before, on or after 1 April 1990.

EW Act sch 3
paras 5,6
EW reg 24

11.14 The penalty should be paid to the authority that imposed it or to the authority of the registration officer who imposed it. Penalties may be collected or recovered by the authority as if they were amounts of community charge. The penalty may be added to any demand notice after the penalty has been imposed. Alternatively the authority may serve notice on the person. Payment will be required within 14 days or such longer period as the authority may allow.

EW reg 24

11.15 No penalty is payable whilst it is the subject of appeal or arbitration.

Penalties in Scotland

S Act ss 17,18A **11.16** The registration officer may require a responsible person (para. 8.29) or an individual who is, has been or is about to be, resident in the registration officer's area to supply reasonably required information. A civil penalty of £50 is imposed upon the responsible person or individual if he or she:

☐ fails to provide the information within a specified period of not less than 21 days; or

☐ provides false information.

11.17 A penalty must not be imposed if the individual has a reasonable excuse. Each time the same failure is repeated a penalty of £200 is imposed.

11.18 An appeal can be made against the imposition of a penalty to the Sheriff. The authority may recover penalties as if they are arrears of community charge.

S Act s 17   **11.19** The registration officer may, in the light of previously unconsidered information, cancel a penalty. This may only be done if an appeal has not been made. Any such penalty paid by a responsible person to an authority must be refunded.

Interest and surcharge

S Act s 18   **11.20** In Scotland anyone who is liable for the personal or standard charge on or after 1 April 1989 who is not registered must:

☐ notify the registration officer within one month of being liable;

☐ provide the information which the registration officer requires to make the entry in the register.

11.21 Everyone who is registered, including collective chargepayers, must notify the registration officer of any change that would require the register entry to be amended.

11.22 If the period between the occurrence of the initial liability, or a change, and its notification to the registration officer is greater than a month then, unless the chargepayer has a reasonable excuse, 10 per cent interest is payable on the amount of charge due after that month and up to the day the new or amended entry is made.

11.23 If the period is greater than 3 months, and the chargepayer has no reasonable excuse for the delay in notifying the registration officer, a surcharge of 30 per cent on the total amount due, or £50, which ever is the greater, also becomes due.

Example

The chargepayer is registered by the authority after 250 days of avoidance. The community charge payable is £315. The amount he must pay is:

☐　daily charge is £0.863 (i.e. $\frac{£315}{365}$)

☐　arrears = £0.863 × 250 = £215.75
☐　interest £0.863 × 220 = £189.86 × 10% = £18.99
☐　surcharge £215.75 × 30% = £64.72
☐　total amount payable = £299.46

11.24 Backdated community charge payments together with payments of interest and surcharge are treated as arrears of community charge. Additionally, of course, the chargepayer must pay the full amount of the personal charge for the remainder of the financial year.

11.25 The chargepayer may appeal to the Sheriff against the imposition of interest or a surcharge (para. 12.13).

11.26 The levying authority must account to the district authority for any interest payments which relate to the district's community charges.

Enforcement

11.27 Enforcement action may be initiated 14 days after the issue of a reminder if payment has not been made. This is the minimum statutory period. In practice no authority attempts to meet it. In England and Wales the authority initiates enforcement action by obtaining a liability order. In Scotland the authority petitions the Sheriff for a summary warrant to recover the arrears. Any enforcement action stops if the outstanding debt (including costs, etc) is paid.

11.28 The introduction of the community charge has imposed an additional cost upon many low income households. As a matter of good practice authorities should ensure that both before, and during, the enforcement process they seek to maximise the relief and benefit awarded to chargepayers (see in particular Chapter 7). Authorities should also bear in mind the additional costs that are imposed upon chargepayers once legal action has been taken to recover arrears. Where ever possible achievable payment arrangements should be negotiated with the chargepayer in place of costly legal action.

11.29 Table 11.1 summarises the enforcement powers available to an English and Welsh authority if payment has not been made.

Table 11.1

ENFORCEMENT ACTION IN ENGLAND AND WALES IF NO PAYMENT IS MADE (PERSONAL AND STANDARD CHARGE)

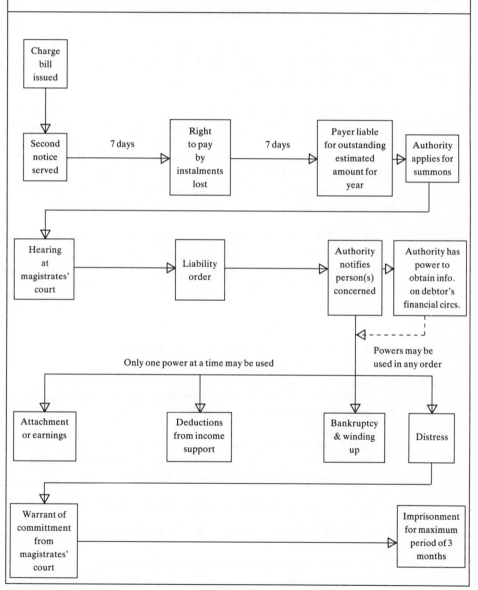

11.30 The following paragraphs first describe the enforcement powers in England and Wales (paras 11.31–79) and then in Scotland (paras 11.80–89). Deduction from income support (para. 11.58) is a remedy available throughout Great Britain.

Liability orders

EW Act sch 4
part 2 para 3
EW reg 29

11.31 The English or Welsh authority may obtain a liability order by application to the magistrates' court. If granted this provides the authority with a range of enforcement powers (para. 11.39).

11.32 A liability order cannot be obtained for an amount that has been due for over 2 years. The authority's application for an order is initiated by complaint to a Justice of the Peace or justice's clerk requesting the issue of a summons to the chargepayer. It informs the chargepayer of the time and date of the hearing and requires that he or she appear before the court and show why the outstanding amount has not been paid.

EW reg 48

11.33 A liability order against a chargepayer may also include those who are jointly and severally liable with the chargepayer, i.e. a partner or a management agent; if reminder has been served on them. A liability order cannot be made against such people alone.

SERVICE OF SUMMONS

EW reg 30

11.34 Summons must be served by one of the following methods:

☐ delivering it to the person concerned; or
☐ leaving it at his or her usual or last known place of abode; or
☐ posting it to that person at his or her usual or last known address; or
☐ in the case of a company delivery to its registered office;
☐ leaving it at, or sending it to, an address given by the person as an address at which service will be accepted.

GROUNDS FOR A LIABILITY ORDER

EW reg 29

11.35 An order must be made if the magistrates are satisfied that:

☐ the sum is payable by the person concerned; and
☐ has not been paid.

11.36 The practice note *Enforcement of the Community Charge*, (PN No. 15, paras 2.7–2.8) summarises the matters on which the authority must satisfy the court if an order is to be made:

☐ the community charge has been fixed by resolution of the authority (para. 13.32);

☐ an entry appears on the community charge register;

☐ the amount due has been demanded in accordance with the statutory provisions (Chapter 10);

☐ full payment of the amount due has not been made by the due date;

☐ a second 'reminder' notice has been issued;

☐ the sum has not been paid within 7 days of the second 'reminder' notice;

☐ a proper summons has been served for the remaining year's outstanding charge at least 7 days after it became payable;

☐ the full sum claimed including costs has not been paid.

DEFENCES AGAINST A LIABILITY ORDER

11.37 The defences available to the chargepayer are:

☐ that he or she was not on the community charge register for the relevant period;

☐ the charge has not been demanded in accordance with the Act and regulations;

☐ the amount has been paid;

☐ the amount is not in accordance with the register entry;

☐ the person is entered on the register of 2 or more authorities, one is the subject of an appeal, and the due amount in the area where he or she was first registered has been paid.

11.38 A dispute about the amount of community charge benefit due is not a defence against a liability order. However, PN No. 15 (para. 2.10) identifies that a court is unlikely to award a liability order while a community charge benefit determination is the subject of a review. Issues such as the chargepayer's exemption from liability are matters which should be taken up at an earlier stage via the appeals process (Chapter 12). They do not constitute a valid defence against the issue of a liability order. The authority may apply for a liability order whilst an appeal is pending. The one exception to this rule is where the appeal is on the grounds that the chargepayer has paid a community charge to another authority (para. 12.6).

THE ORDER

EW regs 29,30
sch 3 Form B

11.39 The liability order is for the amount payable and the authority's reasonably incurred costs. It must be in the form specified in the regulations. The order provides the authority with the following enforcement powers:

☐ a power to obtain financial information about the person(s) concerned;
☐ distress;
☐ attachment of earnings;
☐ deductions from income support;
☐ charging orders (for collective charges only); and
☐ bankruptcy and winding up.

Relationship between remedies

EW reg 46

11.40 The authority may decide in each case which power to use and the order in which to use them. Except for the first power only one of the above powers can be used at any one time. Once the court issues a warrant for committment of a person in debt (para. 11.73) no further action may be taken against that person.

Power to obtain financial information about the person concerned

EW reg 31

11.41 Once an English or Welsh authority has obtained a liability order, and if the amount outstanding remains unpaid, the authority may require the person in debt to supply the following information.

☐ name and address of the debtor's employer;
☐ debtor's (expected) earnings;
☐ (expected) deductions from those earnings for
  – income tax;

- class 1 NI contributions;
- any other attachment of earnings orders;
- the debtor's work or employment identity number or such other information as will enable the employer to identify the debtor;
☐ other sources of income;
☐ whether there is anyone jointly liable with the debtor.

11.42 This action is usually the first step in the enforcement process but it is not a necessary one. The authority's request must be in writing. The person in debt only has to supply information that is within his or her possession or control. The information must be supplied within 14 days of the written request having been made. If the debtor fails without reasonable excuse to supply it, or makes a false statement, he or she is liable on summary conviction to a fine of up to £100 for the former offence and £400 for the latter offence.

Attachment of earning order (AEO)

EW regs 32,36 **11.43** An AEO is an order made by the authority. It instructs the debtor's employer to make deductions from the debtor's earnings and pay the deductions to the authority. A copy of the order must also be sent to the person in debt. An AEO is only of use to the authority if the person in debt is in regular employment. Furthermore the deductions made under the order may well be less than the charge that is payable. Authorities should be aware that in certain cases an AEO may lead to the debtor being dismissed from his or her employment.

11.44 An employer who fails to comply with an AEO is guilty of a criminal offence and subject to a fine not exceeding £400.

11.45 A model instruction form is contained in Appendix A of PN No 15, *Enforcement of the Community Charge*. Authorities may, however, devise their own forms. The AEO must specify:

☐ the amount owing;
☐ the rate of deductions;
☐ the period within which amounts deducted should be paid to the authority.

DEDUCTIONS

EW regs 27,33 **11.46** Deductions are made from net earnings. Earnings are:

☐   any sums payable by way of wages or salary;

☐   fees, bonuses, commission, overtime pay or other emoluments payable in addition to wages or salary, or payable under a contract of service; and by way of pension, including an annuity; and

☐   periodical payments by way of compensation for the loss, abolition or relinquishment, or diminution of the emoluments, of any office or employment.

11.47 Net earnings are gross earnings minus income tax and primary class 1 NI contributions. Pension contributions are not deducted.

EW reg 33, sch 4

11.48 The employer must make deductions in accordance with Table 11.2. These should be contained in the AEO. These Tables can be changed by order of the Secretary of State at any time. In most instances use of the tables is straightforward. The employer finds the band in column 1 which corresponds to the net earnings due to the debtors on the next pay-day. The amount on the same line in column 2 is the amount deducted and paid to the authority.

EW reg 33 sch 4

Table 11.2

DEDUCTIONS TO BE MADE UNDER ATTACHMENT OF EARNINGS ORDER

DEDUCTIONS FROM WEEKLY EARNINGS

Net earnings	Deduction
Not exceeding £35	Nil
Exceeding £35 but not exceeding £55	£1
Exceeding £55 but not exceeding £65	£2
Exceeding £65 but not exceeding £75	£3
Exceeding £75 but not exceeding £80	£4
Exceeding £80 but not exceeding £85	£5
Exceeding £85 but not exceeding £90	£6
Exceeding £90 but not exceeding £95	£7
Exceeding £95 but not exceeding £100	£8
Exceeding £100 but not exceeding £110	£9
Exceeding £110 but not exceeding £120	£11
Exceeding £120 but not exceeding £130	£12
Exceeding £130 but not exceeding £140	£14
Exceeding £140 but not exceeding £150	£15
Exceeding £150 but not exceeding £160	£18
Exceeding £160 but not exceeding £170	£20
Exceeding £170 but not exceeding £180	£23
Exceeding £180 but not exceeding £190	£25
Exceeding £190 but not exceeding £200	£28
Exceeding £200 but not exceeding £220	£35
Exceeding £220 but not exceeding £240	£42
Exceeding £240 but not exceeding £260	£50
Exceeding £260 but not exceeding £280	£59
Exceeding £280 but not exceeding £300	£68
Exceeding £300	£68 in respect of the first £300 plus 50% of the remainder.

Table 11.2, continued

DEDUCTIONS FROM MONTHLY EARNINGS

Net earnings	Deduction
Not exceeding £152	Nil
Exceeding £152 but not exceeding £220	£5
Exceeding £220 but not exceeding £260	£8
Exceeding £260 but not exceeding £280	£11
Exceeding £280 but not exceeding £300	£14
Exceeding £300 but not exceeding £320	£18
Exceeding £320 but not exceeding £340	£21
Exceeding £340 but not exceeding £360	£24
Exceeding £360 but not exceeding £380	£27
Exceeding £380 but not exceeding £400	£30
Exceeding £400 but not exceeding £440	£36
Exceeding £440 but not exceeding £480	£42
Exceeding £480 but not exceeding £520	£48
Exceeding £520 but not exceeding £560	£54
Exceeding £560 but not exceeding £600	£60
Exceeding £600 but not exceeding £640	£66
Exceeding £640 but not exceeding £680	£75
Exceeding £680 but not exceeding £720	£85
Exceeding £720 but not exceeding £760	£95
Exceeding £760 but not exceeding £800	£105
Exceeding £800 but not exceeding £900	£135
Exceeding £900 but not exceeding £1,000	£170
Exceeding £1,000 but not exceeding £1,100	£207
Exceeding £1,100 but not exceeding £1,200	£252
Exceeding £1,200 but not exceeding £1,300	£297
Exceeding £1,300	£297 in respect of the first £1,300 plus 50% of the remainder.

Table 11.2, continued

DEDUCTIONS BASED ON DAILY EARNINGS

Net earnings	Deduction
Not exceeding £5	Nil
Exceeding £5 but not exceeding £9	£0.20
Exceeding £9 but not exceeding £11	£0.50
Exceeding £11 but not exceeding £13	£1.00
Exceeding £13 but not exceeding £15	£1.20
Exceeding £15 but not exceeding £17	£1.40
Exceeding £17 but not exceeding £19	£1.70
Exceeding £19 but not exceeding £21	£2.10
Exceeding £21 but not exceeding £23	£2.50
Exceeding £23 but not exceeding £25	£3.00
Exceeding £25 but not exceeding £27	£3.60
Exceeding £27 but not exceeding £30	£4.50
Exceeding £30 but not exceeding £33	£5.30
Exceeding £33 but not exceeding £36	£6.70
Exceeding £36 but not exceeding £39	£8.00
Exceeding £39 but not exceeding £42	£9.40
Exceeding £42	£9.40 in respect of the first £42 plus 50% of the remainder.

EW reg 34   **11.49** In addition to the amount deducted and paid to the authority employers may deduct £1 from the employee every time a deduction is made to meet their administrative costs. This is particularly punitive for debtors who are paid on a daily basis.

EMPLOYER'S DUTY TO NOTIFY EMPLOYEE THAT DEDUCTIONS HAVE BEEN MADE

EW reg 34   **11.50** Every time the employer makes a deduction under an AEO the employee must be supplied with a written statement of the total amount deducted to date. This must include the £1 deductions to meet the employer's administrative costs. This statement must be provided with the next pay statement after deduction. If a pay statement is not normally issued the statement of deductions must be supplied as soon as possible after the deduction is made. If the employer fails to provide this statement he or she can be prosecuted and fined.

DEBTOR DOES NOT WORK FOR EMPLOYER OR LEAVES EMPLOYER'S EMPLOYMENT

EW reg 34   **11.51** The employer must inform the authority within 14 days of receipt of the AEO if the debtor does not work for him or her or if the debtor leaves the employer's employment. If the employer fails to do this, he or she is liable to a fine.

EW reg 34   **11.52** Anyone who becomes the debtor's employer and knows that an AEO is in force, must notify the authority within 14 days of that fact. The notification must be in writing. If the employer fails to do this he or she is liable to a fine.

DEBTOR'S DUTIES

EW reg 35   **11.53** Whilst the AEO is in force the person in debt must notify the authority in writing, within 14 days, whenever he or she:

☐ leaves an employment;
☐ becomes employed or re-employed.

11.54 In the latter case the letter to the authority must include a statement of:

☐ (expected) earnings;
☐ (expected) deductions for income tax, primary class 1 NI contributions;
☐ the name and address of the employer;
☐ work or employment number.

The authority will send the debtor's new employer a copy of the AEO. If the debtor fails in these duties or provides a statement which contains relevant false information, the offence is punishable with a fine.

END OF THE ORDER

EW reg 36   **11.55** The order remains in force until:

- [ ] the amount is paid by attachment of earnings or some other method;
- [ ] the debtor leaves the employment; or
- [ ] the authority ends (discharges) the order.

The employer must be informed when the AEO has ended.

WHAT HAPPENS WHEN THERE IS MORE THAN ONE AEO?

EW reg 37

11.56 If the employer is already making deductions under another AEO he or she should not make a deduction under an AEO for a community charge debt. The employer should inform the authority that such deductions from earnings are already taking place.

EW reg 37

11.57 If the employer puts into effect a community charge AEO and a second order is later served this should only be put into effect if it was made by a court under the Attachment of Earnings Act 1971. The order says if this is the case. In making such an order the court has a duty to consider the debtor's circumstances including the fact that there is an existing AOE before deciding upon the amount to be deducted. The attachable earnings for such an order are those that remain after the deduction for the first order.

Deductions from income support

EW Act sch 4
para 6
S Act sch 2
para 7A

11.58 If the debtor is in receipt of income support the authority may apply to his or her local DSS office for deductions to be made from that income support. To the authority this process has the advantage of guaranteeing payment. Often, however, the amount received is significantly less than the amount due. Additionally, authorities should bear in mind that income support is a benefit designed to meet the claimant's most basic daily needs. Deductions may not only force the debtor below the poverty line but also into unacceptable levels of hardship.

11.59 The authority's application for deduction must include:

- [ ] the name, address and date of birth of the debtor named in the liability order and of any partner named in the same liability order;
- [ ] the name and place of the court and the date the liability order was obtained;

□   the arrears specified in the liability order;
□   the amount the charging authority wish to deduct.

11.60 Deductions can only be made where the claimant is named in the liability order. The maximum amount the DSS is allowed to deduct for single people is 5 per cent of the income support personal allowance for single people over 25 (Table 7.2) – for couples, 5 per cent of the highest income support personal allowance for a couple (Table 7.2).

11.61 Deductions for arrears of community charge have a lower priority than deductions for housing or fuel costs. The DSS are only allowed to deduct amounts if the claimant is left with 10p in payment after the deduction has been made. Deduction can be made for only one liability order at a time.

11.62 The claimant has the right to appeal to a social security appeal tribunal about decisions relating to deductions for community charge arrears.

Charging orders

EW regs 44,45   **11.63** These apply only in the case of unpaid collective charge. The authority may apply to the county court where the landlord's debt is more than £1,000. The court considers the debtor's circumstances and whether anyone else would be unduly prejudiced by the making of the order. If an order is granted it gives the authority a charge on the property designated for the collective community charge. This means that if it were sold the authority is automatically entitled to receive the outstanding amount from the proceeds of the sale. This is only the case, however, if there is sufficient equity remaining after any charge with a higher priority (e.g. a building society mortgage) has been redeemed.

Bankruptcy and winding up

EW Act sch 4   **11.64** Where a liability order has been obtained, an outstanding
paras 9,10   community charge debt is deemed to be a debt for the purposes of either section 267 of the Insolvency Act 1986 (where the debtor is an individual) or section 122(1)(f) (where the debtor is a company). This means that the authority can present a creditor's petition for

bankruptcy in the case of an individual or petition for the winding up of a company.

11.65 Being made bankrupt in respect of a previous unpaid community charge liability does not affect the bankrupt individual's ongoing community charge liability.

Distress

EW reg 39

11.66 The English or Welsh authority may use distress or distraint. This enables it to seize the debtor's possessions from anywhere in England or Wales and sell them to pay off the outstanding amount plus the charges associated with the levying of distress. Distress may only be levied on certain goods and personal belongings. Other goods such as the clothes or bedding of the debtor or a member of his or her family, or the tools and implements of the debtor's trade not exceeding £150 in value, are protected from distress.

11.67 PN No. 15 (para. 4.3) warns that whilst distress is an effective, economic and efficient way of proceeding in rating terms in many cases that arise under the community charge it is not the most appropriate method. In particular where there are a number of adults in the property disputes may arise over who owns which possessions.

EW reg 39

11.68 If, before any goods are seized, the appropriate amount including any costs is paid or offered to the authority, it must accept the amount and not proceed with the levy. Similarly if the goods have been seized but not sold and the appropriate amount plus any costs is paid or offered, the goods must not be sold and must be made available for collection by the debtor.

EW reg 39

11.69 The bailiff levying distress must carry written authorisation from the authority. He or she must show this authorisation to the debtor if requested to do so. The bailiff must leave at the premises where distress is levied:

☐   a copy of SI 1989 No. 438, regulation 39 and schedule 5;
☐   the charges connected with distress;
☐   a memorandum setting out the appropriate amount; and
☐   hand to the debtor a copy of any close or walking possession agreement entered into.

11.70 Walking possession refers to the circumstance where the authority takes possession of the goods but agrees that it will not remove and sell them until a later date. This later removal and sale only takes place if the debtor has still not paid the appropriate amount. Close possession is the same except someone is left on the premises in physical possession of the goods.

EW reg 39   **11.71** Any defect in the liability order does not make the act of distress illegal or the bailiff a trespasser.

APPEAL AGAINST DISTRESS

EW reg 40   **11.72** A person aggrieved – who may be the debtor or anyone else who is materially affected – by the levy distress (or the attempted levy distress) may appeal to a magistrates' court. An appeal is initiated by a complaint to a Justice of the Peace or justices' clerk requesting that a summons be issued to the authority which levied the distress. If the appeal is successful the court may require the release of distrained goods or payment of compensation where goods have been sold. Additionally if the court is satisfied that the attempted levy was irregular it may order the authority to stop levying in that manner.

Commitment to prison

EW reg 41   **11.73** As a final remedy the authority may apply to the magistrates' court for a warrant committing the debtor to prison. The Scottish legislation contains no equivalent provision.

11.74 This application may only be made if the authority has:

☐ obtained a liability order; and
☐ attempted to levy distress but have found no (or insufficient) goods on which to levy the amount.

11.75 PN No. 15 (para. 7.1) advises that an authority which has not attempted any remedy other than distress should satisfy itself that none of the other available remedies would prove more effective.

11.76 The court must enquire into the debtor's financial circumstances. A warrant of commitment is issued only if the court is satisfied that the debtor's failure to pay is due to his or her:

☐   wilful refusal; or
☐   culpable neglect.

11.77 The maximum period of imprisonment is 3 months. However, the court may fix a term of imprisonment but postpone the issue of the warrant for such time and on such conditions as the court may decide. These conditions will normally include the debtor entering into an agreement to pay. The court has powers to reduce all or part of the amount due.

11.78 Where a person has been committed to prison and:

☐   the whole of the outstanding amount is paid – he or she is released; or
☐   part of the outstanding amount is paid – his or her sentence is reduced on a proportionate basis.

EW reg 46   **11.79** The liability must be written off after the committment to prison as no further enforcement action can be taken.

Summary warrant

S Act sch 2   **11.80** Unlike liability orders, summary warrants are not applied for
para 7   separately. A summary warrant includes all the names, addresses etc. of the defaulter. A Scottish authority obtains a summary warrant by presenting a certificate to the Sheriff. This must state that:

☐   the persons specified in the application have not paid the specified community charge;
☐   the authority has given written notice to each person requiring payment of the account due within 14 days;
☐   the 14-day period has expired; and
☐   specifying the amounts due and unpaid by each person.

11.81 There is no provision for the chargepayer to make representations against the granting of the warrant. The Sheriff has no discretion and must grant a summary warrant on presentation of a certificate.

11.82 Upon the grant of a summary warrant a surcharge of 10 per cent is added to the amount due. Once a summary warrant is granted, each defaulter is sent a summary warrant notice demanding immediate settlement. If the debt remains unpaid it is passed to a Sheriff officer who can pursue the following remedies:

☐ poinding and sale;
☐ earnings arrestment;
☐ arrestment of money or goods held by a third party and their sale;
☐ deductions from income support.

11.83 These procedures must be carried out by a firm of Sheriff Officers. The costs associated with particular remedies are also added to the amount due.

Earnings arrestment

S Act sch 2
para 7

11.84 In Scotland earnings arrestment is a similar process to the English and Welsh attachment of earnings order (para. 11.43) but the process is carried out under the provisions of the Debtors (Scotland) Act 1987. The same reservations may be expressed about its use however (para. 11.43). No separate action is required in the Sheriff's court. The Sheriff Officer lodges an earnings arrestment with the debtor's employer. The employer must make the deductions from the employees earnings in accordance with Table 11.3. which is from Schedule 2 to the Debtors (Scotland) Act 1987. Employers may make a charge of 50p for each deduction.

Table 11.3

DEDUCTIONS FROM EARNINGS: SCOTLAND

DEDUCTIONS FROM WEEKLY EARNINGS

Net earnings	*Deduction*
Not exceeding £35	Nil
Exceeding £35 but not exceeding £40	£1
Exceeding £40 but not exceeding £45	£2
Exceeding £45 but not exceeding £50	£3
Exceeding £50 but not exceeding £55	£4
Exceeding £55 but not exceeding £60	£5
Exceeding £60 but not exceeding £65	£6
Exceeding £65 but not exceeding £70	£7
Exceeding £70 but not exceeding £75	£8
Exceeding £75 but not exceeding £80	£9
Exceeding £80 but not exceeding £85	£10
Exceeding £85 but not exceeding £90	£11
Exceeding £90 but not exceeding £95	£12
Exceeding £95 but not exceeding £100	£13
Exceeding £100 but not exceeding £110	£15
Exceeding £110 but not exceeding £120	£17
Exceeding £120 but not exceeding £130	£19
Exceeding £130 but not exceeding £140	£21
Exceeding £140 but not exceeding £150	£23
Exceeding £150 but not exceeding £160	£26
Exceeding £160 but not exceeding £170	£29
Exceeding £170 but not exceeding £180	£32
Exceeding £180 but not exceeding £190	£35
Exceeding £190 but not exceeding £200	£38
Exceeding £200 but not exceeding £220	£46
Exceeding £220 but not exceeding £240	£54
Exceeding £240 but not exceeding £260	£63
Exceeding £260 but not exceeding £280	£73
Exceeding £280 but not exceeding £300	£83
Exceeding £300	£83 in respect of the first £300 plus 50% of the remainder.

Table 11.3, continued

DEDUCTIONS FROM MONTHLY EARNINGS

Net earnings	*Deduction*
Not exceeding £152	Nil
Exceeding £152 but not exceeding £170	£5
Exceeding £170 but not exceeding £185	£8
Exceeding £185 but not exceeding £200	£11
Exceeding £200 but not exceeding £220	£14
Exceeding £220 but not exceeding £240	£18
Exceeding £240 but not exceeding £260	£22
Exceeding £260 but not exceeding £280	£26
Exceeding £280 but not exceeding £300	£30
Exceeding £300 but not exceeding £320	£34
Exceeding £320 but not exceeding £340	£38
Exceeding £340 but not exceeding £360	£42
Exceeding £360 but not exceeding £380	£46
Exceeding £380 but not exceeding £400	£50
Exceeding £400 but not exceeding £440	£58
Exceeding £440 but not exceeding £480	£66
Exceeding £480 but not exceeding £520	£74
Exceeding £520 but not exceeding £560	£82
Exceeding £560 but not exceeding £600	£90
Exceeding £600 but not exceeding £640	£98
Exceeding £640 but not exceeding £680	£109
Exceeding £680 but not exceeding £720	£121
Exceeding £720 but not exceeding £760	£133
Exceeding £760 but not exceeding £800	£145
Exceeding £800 but not exceeding £900	£180
Exceeding £900 but not exceeding £1,000	£220
Exceeding £1,000 but not exceeding £1,100	£262
Exceeding £1,100 but not exceeding £1,200	£312
Exceeding £1,200 but not exceeding £1,300	£362
Exceeding £1,300	£362 in respect of the first £1,300 plus 50% of the remainder.

Table 11.3, continued

DEDUCTIONS BASED ON DAILY EARNINGS

Net earnings	Deduction
Not exceeding £5	Nil
Exceeding £5 but not exceeding £6	£0.15
Exceeding £6 but not exceeding £7	£0.30
Exceeding £7 but not exceeding £8	£0.45
Exceeding £8 but not exceeding £9	£0.60
Exceeding £9 but not exceeding £10	£1.00
Exceeding £10 but not exceeding £11	£1.20
Exceeding £11 but not exceeding £12	£1.40
Exceeding £12 but not exceeding £13	£1.60
Exceeding £13 but not exceeding £14	£1.80
Exceeding £14 but not exceeding £15	£2.00
Exceeding £15 but not exceeding £17	£2.40
Exceeding £17 but not exceeding £19	£2.70
Exceeding £19 but not exceeding £21	£3.20
Exceeding £21 but not exceeding £23	£3.70
Exceeding £23 but not exceeding £25	£4.30
Exceeding £25 but not exceeding £27	£5.00
Exceeding £27 but not exceeding £30	£6.00
Exceeding £30 but not exceeding £33	£7.00
Exceeding £33 but not exceeding £36	£8.50
Exceeding £36 but not exceeding £39	£10.00
Exceeding £39 but not exceeding £42	£11.50
Exceeding £42	£11.50 in respect of the first £42 plus 50% of the remainder.

Arrestment of money or goods held by a third party

11.85 Arrestment is the means by which a Scottish authority may attach money or goods belonging to the debtor which are held by a third party. For example, money a bank holds for the debtor in his or her bank account. There is no English or Welsh equivalent. Arrestment must be served by the Sheriff Officers serving a schedule on the arrestee, e.g. the bank. General arrestments are served on the main banks, i.e. the Clydesdale, Bank of Scotland, Royal Bank of Scotland and the Trustee Savings Bank; in the hope that the debtor has an account with one of them. A very limited number of items cannot be arrested. These include money payable by the Crown on account of a National Savings Bank Deposit; tools and wearing apparel, books, documents and evidence.

11.86 Arrestment freezes the funds and they cannot be withdrawn until the debt has been settled. Usually the debtor is asked to sign a mandate in favour of the authority for an amount equal to the arrears and costs. This is then transferred to the authority. Any money that remains in the account is released. Where a mandate is not signed a second court order – a furthcoming – has to be obtained to allow arrested funds to be transferred to the authority.

Poinding and sale

S Act sch 2   **11.87** Poinding and sale is the Scottish equivalent of the levying of distress. Certain goods belonging to the debtor are arrested or poinded by the Sheriff Officers. They attach a notional value to each article. The goods are then removed at a later date and sold at the values attached. Most authorities only use this method as a last resort. In practice its use must usually be approved by councillors.

11.88 If the poinded articles are removed without the written consent of the authority, Sheriff Officer or the authorisation of the Sheriff, it is a breach of the poinding. It may be dealt with as contempt of court and could lead to a fine or possible imprisonment.

11.89 Schedule 5 to the Debtors (Scotland) Act specifies a range of items that are exempt from poinding. These are listed in Table 11.4.

Table 11.4

ARTICLES EXEMPT FROM POINDING

Any of the following items that are reasonably required for the use of members of the household cannot be poinded:

☐ clothing;
☐ items required for the practice of a profession, trade or business providing they are not valued at more than £500 in total;
☐ educational or training items providing they are not valued at more than £500 in total;
☐ a child's toys;
☐ articles for the care and upbringing of a child;
☐ furniture, equipment or utensils used for the cooking, storing or eating food;
☐ furniture used for storing clothing, bedding or household linen; cleaning articles, cooking or eating utensils;
☐ beds or bedding; household linen; chairs or settees; tables; food; lights or light fittings; heating appliances; curtains; floor coverings; refrigerators; articles for cleaning, mending or pressing clothes; domestic cleaning items; tools used for the maintenance or repair of the home or of household articles; safety articles, e.g. fire extinguisher.

CHAPTER 12

Appeals

12.1 The community charge can be complicated, and decisions often leave people dissatisfied. This chapter describes how to appeal against them. It covers:

☐ what questions the community charge appeal system applies to;
☐ how to appeal in England and Wales; and
☐ how to appeal in Scotland.

Overview

12.2 The community charge appeal system is fairly straightforward and easy to use, but is designed only to apply to a particular group of community charge questions (Table 12.1). For those questions, there are 2 stages. The first is an appeal to whoever made the decision (the registration officer or the authority itself). The second stage provides an independent appeal: to the Valuation and Community Charge Tribunal in England and Wales, to the Sheriff in Scotland. In some Scottish cases, however, the first stage is omitted: the appeal goes straight to the Sheriff. In some cases it is also possible to appeal to the courts.

Table 12.1

QUESTIONS COVERED BY THE COMMUNITY CHARGE
APPEAL SYSTEM

☐ Appeals about whether a community charge is due at all, or about other aspects of register entries.
☐ Appeals about being left off the public extract (Scotland only).
☐ Appeals about being designated as a responsible person.
☐ Appeals about being designated as a certification officer (England and Wales only).
☐ Appeals about penalties and (in Scotland only) surcharges and interest on backdated charges.
☐ Appeals about the amount of a bill.

WHO CAN APPEAL?

12.3 Anyone can appeal about the community charge decisions described in this chapter. In Scotland, only the person directly affected by the decision can appeal (e.g. the person challenging a register entry must be the person named in that entry, etc). In England and Wales, an appeal may be taken by an 'aggrieved person', which has a wider significance. For example, it is possible for the resident of a short-stay hostel to appeal against a decision that the landlord must administer the collective community charge and contributions; whereas in Scotland only the landlord can do this.

12.4 The person asking for the appeal (or 'appellant') can do so personally, or ask a representative to deal with it on his or her behalf, though legal aid is not available at any stage, except where an appeal goes to the High Court or Court of Session. It is also possible for a group of appellants to ask for identical subject-matters to be dealt with on a combined basis (*Community Charge Appeals*, PN No. 7, para. 3.2).

LIABILITY TO PAY PENDING APPEAL

S Act s 16 sch 2 **12.5** Someone who appeals still has to pay any community charge said to be due, whilst he or she is waiting for the outcome of the appeal. This does not, however, apply to penalties, which are suspended during the course of an appeal. In England and Wales, if someone does not pay his or her community charge whilst waiting for an appeal, it is possible for the authority to take enforcement action over the arrears. However, it would usually be good practice for authorities to suspend such action until the appeal is decided. In Scotland, enforcement action is not allowed if an appeal is pending.

EW reg 19
S Act s 16

12.6 There is an exception to the above rule. If someone appears in 2 or more authorities' registers as having to pay a personal charge, only one is due. This only applies if he or she appeals against at least one of the register entries, and lasts until the appeal is dealt with (including cases where the appeal goes on to the courts), or abandoned, or fails for want of prosecution. Until then, the person has to pay only the personal charge relating to the first register entry made. In England and Wales, an additional detail is added to this rule, as follows. If more than one entry was made on the first day, the person may choose which one to pay. If he or she fails to do so within 14 days of being notified of those entries, the decision is made by drawing lots.

Questions covered by the appeal system

12.7 The community charge appeal system only covers the questions summarised in Table 12.1. These are dealt with in turn below. Questions not covered by the community charge appeal system can be appealed against differently (paras 12.43, 12.63).

APPEALS ABOUT REGISTER ENTRIES

EW Act s 23
S Act s 16

12.8 The community charge register is the record of everyone who has to pay a charge (Chapter 9). Anyone who appears in it may appeal against being in the register at all, or about the contents of his or her register entry, or about an amendment to it. This may be done when the person first appears in the register, or at any time later on (whether or not there has been a change of circumstances). It is also possible for someone who does not appear in the register to appeal against that.

12.9 A very wide range of appeals is possible here, including appeals about:

☐   where someone's sole or main residence is, in relation to a personal charge;

☐   whether someone is exempt from a personal charge;

☐   whether someone is a registered student;

☐   whether property should be subject to a standard charge;

☐   which class a standard charge property should fall into;

☐   whether property is appropriate for a collective charge;

☐   what dates a person is liable for a community charge.

APPEALS ABOUT BEING LEFT OFF THE PUBLIC EXTRACT

S Act s 20

12.10 People at risk of violence may apply to the registration officer to have their names left off the public extract of the register (paras 9.14 onwards). The community charge appeal system in England and Wales does not apply in these cases (para. 12.44). In Scotland, however, an appeal may be made against an initial refusal by the registration officer to allow anonymous registration, or against a refusal to continue to allow anonymous registration.

APPEALS BY RESPONSIBLE PERSONS

EW Act s 23
S Act s 17

12.11 If the registration officer designates someone as a responsible person for a property in the area, he or she has a duty to give information about the people who live there (para. 8.21). Anyone can appeal against such a designation – even if he or she has already begun to comply with the duties involved. The grounds might be that it is unreasonable for the registration officer to expect him or her to provide information about the other residents there. However, the powers of registration officers to choose who should be a responsible person are wide, and appellants are advised to set out all their reasons clearly.

APPEALS BY CERTIFICATION OFFICERS

EW Act s 23

12.12 If the registration officer designates someone as a certification officer for an educational establishment, he or she has various duties to provide certificates to students, etc (para. 8.35). The person concerned can appeal against this. This only applies in England and Wales, because the law in Scotland does not provide for the existence of certification officers as such.

APPEALS ABOUT PENALTIES, SURCHARGES, ETC

EW Act s 23
S Act ss 17,
18,18A

12.13 The registration officer (or in some cases the authority) may in various circumstances impose penalties on chargepayers and others and, in Scotland, impose surcharges and interest on backdated charges. These apply where the person fails to comply with a requirement imposed on him or her – e.g. to register for the community charge (Chapter 11). Anyone can appeal against these. The grounds can be:

☐ that there was no power to impose them, because there was no failure to comply with the requirement concerned;

☐ that there was no power to impose them, because there was a good reason for failure to comply with the requirement concerned;

☐ that, even where the above do not apply, discretion should have been exercised not to impose them or to subsequently revoke them. This last ground cannot apply in the case of interest on backdated charges since no discretion exists in that case (paras 11.22–23).

APPEALS ABOUT THE AMOUNT OF A BILL

EW Act s 23
EW reg 25
S Act sch 2

12.14 In Scotland, anyone who receives any community charge bill can appeal against the amount, including cases where bills are raised under the provisions relating to joint and several liability of couples, etc (Chapter 10). In England and Wales, someone can appeal against the amount of a bill (including bills in joint and several liability cases), but only where it has been estimated – i.e. where it has been assessed for a future period according to various assumptions that the chargepayer's circumstances will not change (para. 10.20); but the appeal may not challenge the assumptions laid down by law.

12.15 Possible grounds for appeal under this heading are therefore:

☐ against calculation errors (in England, Wales and Scotland); and

☐ against assumptions not laid down by law. This includes all assumptions in Scotland, and a few in England and Wales.

S Act s 19

12.16 If the amount of a bill is wrong because a register entry is incorrect (e.g. someone is not recorded as being a student, but he or she should be), the appeal must be against the register entry (paras 12.8–9), and not against the resultant amount. This is because it is the authority which deals with appeals about bills, and it cannot change register entries; whereas the registration officer (who deals with appeals about register entries) can.

How to appeal in England and Wales

12.17 There are 2 main stages to the community charge appeal system in England and Wales:

☐ the first appeal: 'serving notice' on the registration officer or charging authority;
☐ the second appeal: to a Valuation and Community Charge Tribunal (VCCT).

12.18 After that it may be possible to apply for the VCCT to review its decision, or to appeal to the High Court. The procedure and timetable is outlined in Table 12.2.

Table 12.2

APPEAL PROCEDURE AND TIMETABLE: ENGLAND AND WALES

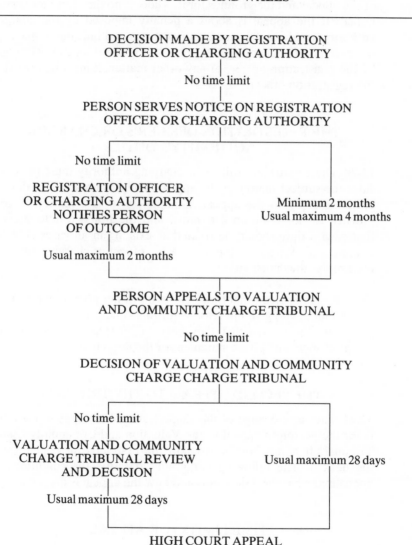

DECISION MADE BY REGISTRATION
OFFICER OR CHARGING AUTHORITY

No time limit

PERSON SERVES NOTICE ON REGISTRATION
OFFICER OR CHARGING AUTHORITY

No time limit

REGISTRATION OFFICER
OR CHARGING AUTHORITY
NOTIFIES PERSON
OF OUTCOME

Minimum 2 months
Usual maximum 4 months

Usual maximum 2 months

PERSON APPEALS TO VALUATION
AND COMMUNITY CHARGE TRIBUNAL

No time limit

DECISION OF VALUATION AND COMMUNITY
CHARGE CHARGE TRIBUNAL

No time limit

VALUATION AND COMMUNITY
CHARGE TRIBUNAL REVIEW
AND DECISION

Usual maximum 28 days

Usual maximum 28 days

HIGH COURT APPEAL

THE FIRST APPEAL: SERVING NOTICE

EW Act s 24   **12.19** The first stage of the English and Welsh appeal procedure is for the appellant to serve notice on the registration officer or charging authority. The notice must be in writing, and state the subject matter of the appeal and the grounds for it. There is no time limit for serving notice. If the appeal is about a penalty imposed by the charging authority, or about the amount of an estimated bill, the notice must be served on the charging authority. If it is about a penalty imposed by the registration officer, or any other matter, it must be served on the registration officer.

THE REGISTRATION OFFICER'S OR CHARGING AUTHORITY'S DUTIES

EW Act s 24   **12.20** The registration officer or charging authority must then consider the subject matter of the appeal. There is no absolute duty on either to reply to the appeal; nonetheless, it is a matter of good practice to do so within 2 months, and the practice note suggests that such a duty should be treated as existing in all cases (PN No. 7, para. 4.3). Whenever the registration officer or charging authority does reply, they must either:

☐ notify the person that they believe his or her grievance is not well founded, and give the reasons for this belief; or

☐ notify the person that they have taken steps to deal with the grievance, and give a statement of the steps taken.

THE SECOND APPEAL: TO THE TRIBUNAL

EW Act s 23   **12.21** The second stage of the English and Welsh appeal procedure is for the person to appeal to the Valuation and Community Charge Tribunal. It is not possible to skip the first stage of appeal (serving notice). The following paragraphs describe the conditions for appealing, what the Tribunal is and how the appeal is dealt with.

TIME LIMITS FOR APPEAL

EW Act s 24
EW SI 1989
No.439

12.22 There are 2 time limits applying to Tribunal appeals:

(a)   if the registration officer or charging authority notifies the appellant in either of the ways described above (para. 12.20), the appellant can appeal to the VCCT within 2 months of the notification (no matter how long it took for the notification to be made);

(b)   if the registration officer or charging authority does not notify the appellant in either of the ways described above, the appellant may appeal to the VCCT at any time between 2 and 4 months after serving written notice.

12.23 If an appellant fails to make an appeal within the time limit in (b), but the registration officer or charging authority subsequently notifies the outcome of their decision, the person then has 2 months from the date of that notification in which to appeal – the time limit in (a).

EW SI 1989
No.439

12.24 In either of the above cases, the president of the VCCT may authorise an appeal to be entertained by the Tribunal if he or she is satisfied that the failure to observe the time limits arose through circumstances beyond the person's control.

OTHER CONDITIONS FOR APPEAL

EW SI 1989
No.439

12.25 The appellant must serve a notice of appeal on the clerk of the Tribunal. The practice note (PN No. 7, section 6) is out of date in saying that there is a prescribed form for appeals. Appeals may be made in any written format, so long as they contain:

☐   the grounds for the appeal;

☐   the date on which the appellant served notice on the registration officer or the charging authority (in the first step of the appeal procedure); and

☐   the date (if any) of the registration officer's or charging authority's reply.

EW SI 1989
No.439

12.26 The clerk notifies the appellant that the appeal has been received and sends a copy to the registration officer or the charging authority concerned (and also to any other registration officer or charging authority who may be concerned).

WITHDRAWING FROM AN APPEAL

EW SI 1989
No.439

12.27 At any time before the appeal is dealt with, the person may withdraw the appeal by notifying the clerk in writing.

WHAT IS A VALUATION AND COMMUNITY CHARGE TRIBUNAL?

EW Act s 136
schs 1,12
EW SI 1989
No.439
EW SI 1989
No.440

12.28 Valuation and Community Charge Tribunals were established on 1 May 1989 as successors to local valuation courts. Their costs are met by Parliament. There are 5 London Tribunals and one (or in some cases 2) for each county in England and Wales. They are under the direct supervision of the Council on Tribunals and exercise jurisdiction over:

☐   community charge appeals; and
☐   appeals in connection with non-domestic rating.

EW SI 1989
No.439

12.29 Tribunal members are appointed by the county council or (in London and the metropolitan counties) the districts and boroughs in the area. The members elect a president (with overall responsibility for securing arrangements for appeals) and various chairmen or chairwomen, and appoint a clerk and any other staff required. Members receive allowances for attendance, etc. In certain cases, members, staff, etc may be disqualified from taking part in a hearing in which they may have an apparent interest: e.g. where they are also councillors of the authority the appeal is against, or where the appellant is the spouse of such a person.

EW SI 1989
No.439

12.30 With 2 exceptions, the Tribunal deals with all appeals in its area. The first exception is when an appellant appears in 2 or more community charge registers as subject to a personal community charge, and appeals against more than one entry. If this would fall to be dealt with by different Tribunals, the appellant may choose which Tribunal is to deal with the appeals. The second exception is where an appeal is initiated by any member of the Tribunal. Such an appeal is dealt with by another Tribunal.

HOW IS THE APPEAL DEALT WITH?

EW SI 1989
No.439

12.31 Appeals may be dealt with by written representations alone, if all the parties agree, and subject to further conditions about the provision of written summaries of each party's case. They may also, if all the parties agree, be referred to arbitration under the Arbitration Act 1950. In all other cases, they are dealt with at a hearing.

HEARINGS

EW SI 1989
No.439

12.32 The clerk of the Tribunal gives 21 days' notice of the hearing to each of the parties. The date, time and place of the hearing is publicly advertised, and a list of cases (other than cases where the appellant has an anonymous register entry) is available for inspection. The parties to the appeal may attend and be assisted by any person or be represented by a lawyer or any other person (though legal aid is not available).

EW SI 1989
No.439

12.33 Three members of the Tribunal undertake the hearing, with a chairman or chairwoman presiding. Two members only (with or without a chairman or chairwoman) are allowed if all the parties agree. The appeal is in public unless one of the parties objects and the Tribunal is satisfied that a public hearing would prejudice one of the parties' case. The appeal may be dismissed if the appellant does not attend. The hearing may continue in the absence of any other party. The Tribunal may decide the order of the hearing, examine and call witnesses, require evidence on oath and postpone or adjourn a hearing. So far as appropriate the Tribunal must 'seek to avoid formality in its proceedings'.

EVIDENCE

EW SI 1989
No.439

12.34 The Tribunal is not bound by the rules of law relating to admissibility of evidence. However, community charge register entries may be proved by the production of a copy certified by the registration officer. The following kinds of information may be introduced as evidence, subject to every party having the right to inspect and take extracts of it:

☐ information obtained by a registration officer under his or her statutory power to require it from responsible persons, others who may be liable for a charge, those whose liability has been missed or whose circumstances have changed, certification officers and public bodies;

☐ information obtained by the registration officer about social security or from another registration officer; and

☐   information obtained by a charging authority under its statutory powers to obtain information.

DECISIONS

EW SI 1989
No.439

12.35 The appeal is decided by a majority of the Tribunal members participating. If only 2 members are present at a hearing and they cannot agree, it is remitted to a differently constituted Tribunal. Decisions may be in writing or oral, though if the appeal was dealt with in writing, the decision must be in writing. Written decisions must be notified as soon as reasonably practicable to the parties.

THE EFFECT OF A DECISION

EW Act sch 11
EW SI 1989
No.439

12.36 Following its decision, the Tribunal may order the registration officer or charging authority (as appropriate):

☐   to alter the community charges register (including revoking a designation that a property is subject to the collective community charge);
☐   to revoke a designation of a person as a responsible individual or a certification officer;
☐   to quash a penalty;
☐   to alter an estimated liability for a charge; and
☐   any ancillary matter.

EW Act sch 11   **12.37** An order by the Tribunal is binding on the registration officer or charging authority. (For example, any resultant overpayment of a community charge must be repaid.)

RECORDS OF DECISIONS

EW SI 1989
No.439

12.38 The clerk of the Tribunal is responsible for recording (in documentary or other form) all decisions and orders and sending a copy to each party. Each record of a decision must contain:

☐   the appellant's name and address;
☐   the date of the appeal;
☐   the matter appealed against;
☐   the name of the charging authority or title of the registration officer concerned;
☐   the date of the hearing or decision;
☐   the names of any parties appearing;

☐   the Tribunal's decision and its date;
☐   the reasons for the decision;
☐   any order made in consequence of the decision; and
☐   the date of any such order.

EW SI 1989
No.439

12.39 Records are open to the inspection of any party to any community charge appeal before a VCCT. Failure to allow such parties to inspect is a criminal offence, unless the person concerned reasonably believes that inspection might incur the risk of physical violence to anyone named in a record. The correction of clerical errors must be authorised by the chairman or chairwoman, and amended records must be sent to each party.

REVIEWS OF TRIBUNAL DECISIONS

EW SI 1989
No.439

12.40 A Tribunal may, on the written application of any party to an appeal, revoke, vary or set aside a decision it has made, but only if:

☐   the decision was wrongly made by clerical error;
☐   a party did not receive notice and did not appear;
☐   new evidence has arisen which could not have been ascertained by reasonably diligent enquiry; or
☐   the interests of justice so require.

12.41 The Tribunal must, as far as reasonably practicable, consist of the same members as that which initially heard the appeal. If a decision is set aside, any resulting order must also be set aside, and a re-hearing must be ordered (which may be heard by the same or a different Tribunal).

APPEALS TO THE HIGH COURT

EW SI 1989
No.439

12.42 Appeals against decisions and orders of a Tribunal may be made to the High Court on a question of law. They may dismissed if not made within 28 days. If all the parties agree, an appeal which would normally be heard by a Tribunal may be heard instead by the High Court (PN No. 7, para. 9.2).

OTHER METHODS OF APPEAL

12.43 The community charge appeal system described above applies only to the questions outlined in paras 12.8–16. In England and Wales, it does not apply in cases such as the following:

- matters relating to debt recovery (though there are other procedures to bear in mind here: Chapter 11);
- failure by the authority to repay an overpayment of community charge (para. 10.15);
- most matters relating to joint and several liability;
- appeals about being left off the public extract (para. 9.14);
- matters relating to community charge benefit and the transitional relief scheme (Chapter 7); and
- certain other matters described below.

12.44 Someone who is dissatisfied with a decision should nonetheless be encouraged to write detailing his or her grounds for disagreement. Most registration officers and authorities will wish to consider these outside the community charge appeal system. In some cases it may be possible to apply for judicial review of a decision, or to invoke the assistance of local councillors or the ombudsman.

EW Act ss 138, 142   **12.45** The process of judicial review before the High Court may be used in challenging many decisions of public bodies. In appropriate circumstances this may apply both to subjects which may be subject to the community charge appeal system, and to subjects which may not. Specifically, the following matters may be challenged only by judicial review:

- the setting by a charging authority of the amount(s) of its personal community charge;
- the determination by a charging authority of any standard community charge multiplier;
- the specification by the Secretary of State of the classes to which different standard community charge multipliers apply;
- a precept issued by a precepting authority;
- a levy issued by a levying body;
- the calculation of a charging authorities' expenses in connection with the setting of its personal community charge; and
- the calculation of a precepting authorities' expenses in connection with the issuing of its precepts.

How to appeal in Scotland

12.46 The community charge appeal system in Scotland has 2 stages for some appeals. For others, the first stage is omitted. Which procedure applies to which kinds of appeal is summarised in Table 12.3. It may also be possible to appeal to the Court of Session (para. 12.62). The 2 stages are:

☐ an appeal to the registration officer (known as a registration apeal) or the authority (known as a levying appeal);
☐ an appeal to the Sheriff.

Table 12.3

SUMMARY OF APPEALS PROCEDURES IN SCOTLAND

Registration appeals

☐ Against the making, amending or deleting of a register entry, or against the contents of an entry.
☐ Against being designated as a responsible person.

Levying appeals

☐ Against the amount of a community charge bill.

Appeals to the Sheriff

☐ Against the outcome of a registration or levying appeal.
☐ Against the refusal (or failure within 2 months) by the registration officer to make, amend or delete a register entry.
☐ About the area in which the person should pay a personal community charge.
☐ Against a penalty, surcharge, interest or backdated community charge.
☐ Against a refusal by the registration officer to allow (or continue to allow) a person to be left off the public list.

REGISTRATION APPEALS

S Act ss 16,17
S SI 1988
No.1539

12.47 There are 2 kinds of appeal known as 'registration appeals':

☐ where the registration officer has notified the appellant of a register entry, amendment or deletion to the register, and he or she disagrees with this or with the contents of the entry (paras 12.8–9);

☐ where the registration officer has designated the appellant as a responsible person, and he or she disagrees (para. 12.11).

S SI 1988
No.1539

12.48 Registration appeals must be made to the registration officer within 28 days of receiving notice that the register entry has been made, amended or deleted; or that he or she has been designated as a responsible person. The appeal must be in writing and:

☐ give the appellant's name and address;

☐ specify the register entry, amendment or deletion against which the appeal is made, or the address of the property for which the appellant has been designated responsible person;

☐ give all the grounds for appeal and any supporting evidence;

☐ be dated;

☐ give the name and address of any other potential interested party of whom the appellant is aware; and

☐ be signed by the appellant or agent (giving, where appropriate the name and address of the latter).

S SI 1988
No.1539

12.49 On receipt of the appeal, the registration officer has 2 options:

☐ to agree the appeal and notify the appellant in writing of that fact; or

☐ to hold a hearing.

REGISTRATION HEARINGS

S SI 1988
No.1539

12.50 If the registration officer decides to hold a hearing, he or she sends a copy of the appeal and various other information to any other potential interested party mentioned by the appellant, and any other potential interested party of whom the registration officer is aware (in the last case, notifying the appellant of those persons). Any such person may make written representations to the registration officer (and must send a copy to the appellant), within 14 days. He or she is then treated as an interested party. The registration officer then notifies the appellant and any interested party of the date of the hearing, giving them at least 14 days' notice in writing.

S SI 1988
No.1539

12.51 The appellant may withdraw from an appeal at any time before the date fixed for the hearing. In such a case, the registration officer must inform all the interested parties accordingly.

S SI 1988
No.1539

12.52 The appellant and any interested party may attend, be represented, and be heard at a private hearing before the registration officer (though legal aid is not available). The registration officer decides the procedure at the hearing, but he or she must take into account the written application for the appeal and any written evidence from interested parties, as well as what the parties at the hearing say. The hearing may proceed in the absence of any or all of the parties.

S SI 1988
No.1539

12.53 The registration officer must determine the appeal within 2 months of the date on which it is lodged, and must immediately notify the appellant and interested parties of the outcome and his or her reasons. If the appellant remains dissatisfied, he or she may appeal to the Sheriff (para. 12.56).

LEVYING APPEALS

S SI 1988
No.1880

12.54 This procedure applies to appeals about the amount of a community charge bill (paras 12.14–16). Such appeals must be made to the levying authority (or housing body if it is acting as an agency for the levying authority) in writing within 28 days of the bill, and must:

☐   give the name and address of the appellant;
☐   refer to the bill to which it relates;
☐   give the reasons for the appeal and any supporting evidence;
☐   be dated;
☐   be signed by the appellant or agent (giving, where appropriate, the name and address of the latter).

12.55 There are no further rules about levying appeals (e.g. as regards time scales for determining them). If the appellant remains dissatisfied with the outcome, he or she may appeal to the Sheriff (para. 12.56).

APPEALS TO THE SHERIFF

S Act ss 16,
20A,29

12.56 Table 12.3 and the following paragraphs summarise the cases where an appeal may be made to the Sheriff. In each case the appeal must be made within 28 days or within such additional time as the Sheriff may allow. The Sheriff's decision is binding on the registration officer (or levying authority).

S Act ss 16,17   **12.57** Anyone who is dissatisfied with the outcome of a registration
sch 2   appeal or levying appeal, may appeal to the Sheriff.

S Act s 16   **12.58** If the registration officer refuses the request of a person to
S SI 1988   make, amend or delete an entry to the register, or fails to reply
No.1539   to such a request within 2 months, the person may appeal to the
                  Sheriff. This is distinct from cases where someone is notified by the
                  registration officer of a register entry, amendment or deletion, which
                  are dealt within in paras 12.47 onwards.

S Act s 16   **12.59** If a question arises about the area in which a person should pay
                  a personal community charge, he or she may appeal to the Sheriff.
                  In such a case, the Sheriff must give all the registration officers
                  concerned the opportunity of taking part in the appeal.

S Act ss 17,18,   **12.60** Anyone can appeal to the Sheriff against the imposition
18A   of a penalty, a surcharge, interest on backdated charges, or the
                  backdating of charges itself. In the last case (backdating), however, it
                  would usually be appropriate to appeal against the register entry first
                  (para. 12.47), rather than going straight to the Sheriff.

S Act s 20A   **12.61** An appeal may be made to the Sheriff against a refusal by the
                  registration officer to allow someone to be left off the public list;
                  and also in cases where the registration officer has decided to end
                  allowing this, the person has applied against this, and the registration
                  officer has refused that application. In these cases, the Sheriff's
                  hearing must be in private unless the Sheriff orders otherwise.

APPEALS TO THE COURT OF SESSION

S Act s 29   **12.62** An appeal against the Sheriff may be made to the Court of
                  Session, but only on a question of law.

OTHER METHODS OF APPEAL

12.63 The community charge appeal system described above applies
only to the questions outlined in paras 12.8–16. In Scotland, it does
not apply in cases such as the following:

☐ matters relating to debt recovery (though there are other procedures to bear in mind here: Chapter 11);

☐ failure by the authority to repay an overpayment of community
   charge (para. 10.15);
☐ most matters relating to joint and several liability;
☐ matters relating to community charge benefit and the transitional
   relief scheme (Chapter 7).

12.64 Someone who is dissatisfied with a decision should nonetheless be encouraged to write, detailing his or her grounds for
disagreement. Most registration officers and authorities will wish to
consider these outside the community charge appeal system. In some
cases it may be possible to apply for judicial review of a decision, or
to invoke the assistance of local councillors or the ombudsman.

12.65 The process of judicial review before the Court of Session
may be used in challenging many decisions of public bodies. In
appropriate circumstances this may apply both to subjects which may
be subject to the community charge appeal system, and to subjects
which may not.

CHAPTER 13

Finance

13.1 The community charge is one component in a new system of authority revenue finance implemented on 1 April 1990. This chapter considers the following:

☐ the funds which must be set up and maintained by English and Welsh authorities;
☐ revenue support grant;
☐ national non-domestic rate;
☐ the setting of an authority's community charge;
☐ the Secretary of State's power to cap the amount of an authority's expenditure met from the community charge or the precept of a non-charging authority.

13.2 The financing of council housing and authority capital expenditure in England and Wales are also the subjects of major change from 1 April 1990 as a result of the Local Government and Housing Act 1989 (see *The Local Government and Housing Act 1989 A Guide To The Housing Aspects*, by Martin Ward).

13.3 Table 13.1 summarises the main components of authority revenue finance in England from 1990. The systems differ in detail in Wales and Scotland. The Welsh revenue grant (para. 13.10) and national non-domestic rates (para. 13.13) are paid separately to Welsh counties and districts and not channelled through one collection fund in each area. There is a different level of national non-domestic rates in Wales and a separate Welsh national non-domestic rates pool. The major reform of revenue finance occurred in Scotland on 1 April 1989. The Scottish system is not covered in detail.

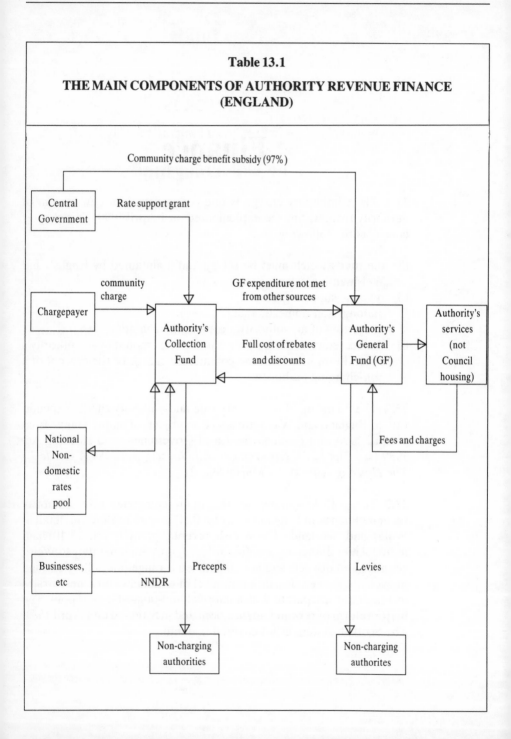

Table 13.1

THE MAIN COMPONENTS OF AUTHORITY REVENUE FINANCE (ENGLAND)

New funds

EW Act ss 89, 91

13.4 Each authority in England and Wales must set up and maintain both:

☐ a collection fund; and
☐ a general fund (or in the City of London, the City Fund).

The collection fund

EW Act ss 90, 98

13.5 The main payments into the English authority's collection fund include:

☐ community charge payments;
☐ transfers from the general fund to meet the full cost of rebates for the community charge and any discounts;
☐ revenue support grant;
☐ national non-domestic rates:
   – less (in certain instances) contributions to the national pool;
   – plus (in other instances) payments from the national pool.

13.6 The main payments out of the English authority's collection fund include:

☐ precepts for other authorities;
☐ the authority's estimate of the amount of money needed to meet its expenditure paid for out of the general fund and not met from other sources, e.g. fees and charges and specific subsidies.

13.7 Separate provision is made for the collection fund in Wales (para. 13.3).

13.8 Central government normally refunds 97 per cent of the authority's expenditure on community charge benefit by way of a specific community charge benefit subsidy. This is paid into the authority's general fund. Where benefit is backdated because the chargepayer has continuous good cause for a late claim (para. 7.55) only 25 per cent subsidy is payable on the backdated element.

13.9 All demands for payment for a year on the fund must be met in full in that year. The operation of the collection fund is described in detail in PN No. 22.

Revenue support grant (RSG)

EW Act part V
S Act s 23
sch 4

13.10 Revenue support grant (RSG) replaces rate support grant (also formerly abbreviated to RSG). It is the main source of central government money to meet the costs of an authority's services. It is not allocated according to an authority's expenditure but according to a centrally determined assessment of the authority's need to spend. RSG is allocated between authorities with the objective of ensuring that if authorities spend at the level of their needs assessment then chargepayers should pay the same amount in every authority. Any spending by an authority above its needs level must be met entirely from its community charge income.

13.11 In Scotland revenue support grant replaced rate support grant in 1989-90.

TRANSITIONAL ARRANGEMENTS

EW Act ss 84,
88A

13.12 Originally the new grant system was to have been phased in over a 4-year period by the application of a safety net, which would have mitigated the losses suffered by some authorities, and a cap which would moderated excessive increases. Now the safety net is to be abolished in the second year of the charge. Gaining authorities no longer have to contribute to the safety net in those years. Instead, an additional grant is paid to the losing authorities to make up the loss of income from the safety net pool.

National non-domestic rates (NNDR)

13.13 A revised form of rating remains for all non-domestic premises, e.g. business premises. In England and Wales the introduction of this system has been preceded by an Inland Revenue revaluation of all non-domestic properties. Future revaluations take place at 5-year intervals after 1990. As with the old system the rates are calculated by multiplying the rateable value by the rate poundage. Unlike the old system, however, the rate poundage (known as a multiplier) is set by central government not the authority. The multiplier is uniform across England.

13.14 For 1990-91 the multiplier is set at a level which, taken together with the revised revaluation figures, approximately generates the same amount of income as non-domestic rates produced in the last year of the old system (1989-90). Future annual increases are linked to the Retail Price Index and cannot rise by more than the rate of inflation.

13.15 Some businesses pay less and some more under the new system. Transitional arrangements limit the gains and losses to any business over the first few years of the new arrangements. Those likely to be worse off are retail outlets in London and the south of England due to the revaluation which reflected disproportionate increases in property values in those parts of the country. Within 6 months of the new valuation list coming into force on 1 April 1990 non-domestic users may propose a change in their rateable value to the valuation officer. If there is no agreement on a revised valuation figure then an appeal can be made to the Valuation and Community Charge Tribunal. After this initial period, proposals and appeals are still possible where a change takes place which affects the value of the property.

NATIONAL NON-DOMESTIC RATES POOL

13.16 The NNDR is collected by individual authorities and is an income to their collection funds. The entitlement of English and Welsh authorities to NNDR, however, is based on their populations. Thus some authorities make a contribution to a national pool and others receive payments from that pool. There is thus a transfer from authorities with a high rateable income and low population to authorities with the opposite characteristics. Special arrangements apply to the City of London.

13.17 A new system of non-domestic rates were introduced in Scotland in 1989-90. In Scotland the Secretary of State sets the maximum figure for non-domestic rates. Authorities however may set a lower level. Scotland is expected to move towards the national pool system over a number of years.

EXEMPTIONS

EW Act s 51
sch 5

13.18 Certain properties are exempt from non-domestic rating. These include premises:

☐ used wholly for, or by, people with disabilities who are registrable under the National Assistance Act 1948; and

☐ places of religious worship.

RELIEFS

13.19 Certain property is eligible for rate relief. In England and Wales mandatory relief of 80 per cent is available to ratepayers that are:

☐ registered, excepted or exempt charities; and who have

☐ property which is wholly or mainly used for charitable purposes.

13.20 This relief is met from offsets against payments into the NNDR pool (i.e. borne nationally by non-domestic rate payers).

13.21 Authorities have the discretion to extend this relief up to 100 per cent. Where this is the case 25 per cent of the additional discretionary relief is met by offsets against payments into the NNDR pool and 75 per cent by chargepayers.

EW Act s 47   **13.22** Authorities also have the discretion to grant relief of up to 100 per cent on property all or part of which is occupied for the purposes of a non-profit making:

☐ institution or other organisation whose main objectives are philanthropic, or religious, or concerned with social welfare, science, literature or the fine arts or;

☐ club, society or other organisation and is used for the purpose of recreation.

13.23 75 per cent of the cost of this relief is met from offsets against payments into the NNDR pool and 25 per cent by chargepayers.

13.24 Applications may be made by writing to the authority's finance/treasurer's department. There is, however, no statutory requirement that applications be made and authorities can take the initiative and grant relief in appropriate circumstances.

13.25 Every request for discretionary relief must be considered on its individual merits. Nevertheless the authority may adopt certain criteria to guide its decision-making. For example, does the organisation have an open access policy? Does it encourage membership from black and ethnic minority groups, women, pensioners and people with disabilities? The theme of good practice in the granting of discretionary relief is further examined in the Department of the Environment and Welsh Office practice note, *Non-domestic Rates: Discretionary Rate Relief.*

EW Act s 49   **13.26** Authorities also have the discretion to provide up to 100 per cent relief from NNDR liability where:

☐   the ratepayer would sustain hardship if the authority was not to do so; and
☐   it is reasonable to do so having regard to the interest of chargepayers.

PRECEPTS

EW Act part IV   **13.27** Precepts are annual demands from certain non-charging authorities which must be met from an authority's collection fund. Precepts must be issued before the 1 March preceding the relevant financial year. Precepting authorities include county councils, metropolitan county police authorities, fire and civil defence authorities, parish and community councils. In setting their community charge authorities must allow for any such precepts.

General fund

EW Act s 91   **13.28** The general fund receives all the income and expenditure of the authority except that which goes through the collection fund, and that related to council housing which goes through a separate housing revenue account (HRA). The authority's general fund receives an amount from its collection fund to meet the authority's estimated expenditure.

Levies

13.29 A levy is issued by certain bodies to meet their annual expenditure. Unlike a precept, a levy may be issued against both a charging and a precepting authority. A charging authority must meet the cost of a levy from its general fund rather than its collection fund. Levying bodies include such organisations as the residuary bodies dealing with the assets and liabilities of the GLC and metropolitan county councils' organisations.

The authority's estimates of its expenditure

EW Act s 95   **13.30** Before the authority can decide the level of its community charge it must budget for its expenditure and income (ignoring any income from the collection fund) in the forthcoming financial year. This must be done by 11 March.

EW Act s 96   **13.31** The authority may recalculate its expenditure at any time, e.g., after a change of political control. This recalculation cannot, however, lead to an increase in the expenditure that must be met from the (collection fund) community charge. The exception to this rule is where the original calculation is quashed because, e.g., it was improperly carried out.

SETTING THE LEVEL OF THE COMMUNITY CHARGE

EW Act s 32   **13.32** The authority sets its community charge at a level necessary
S Act s 9   to meet its likely annual outgoings from the collection fund (paras 13.5–6) after allowing for its other sources of income, such as RSG, NNDR, etc. In Scotland, the charge is set to meet expenses not met by other means.

DIFFERENT PERSONAL COMMUNITY CHARGE AMOUNTS IN THE SAME AUTHORITY

EW Act s 33   **13.33** Usually an authority must set one amount for the personal community charge in its area. However where a precept (e.g. from a parish council) is applicable to only part of an authority's area the amount of personal community charge varies accordingly.

REVISING THE LEVEL OF THE CHARGE

13.34 Where the authority has recalculated its expenditure as described above the authority may set a revised community charge for the year but this need not happen (i.e. any savings may be reflected in the next year's community charge). This revised amount must usually be lower unless the original calculation has been quashed (para. 13.31).

13.35 Scottish authorities have no power to revise the level of their charge.

PUBLICISING THE CHARGE

EW Act s 39   **13.36** Once a charge has been set or revised the authority must publish a note of the amount(s) in at least one newspaper circulating in its area. Unlike former rating law, failure to carry out this duty does not affect the validity of the charge or the chargepayer's liability for it.

Challenging the level of charge

13.37 Where the authority's expenditure is greater than the level estimated by the Secretary of State for revenue support grant purposes, the whole of the additional expenditure must be borne by community chargepayers or by increasing fees, etc, for the service provided. The public may only question the amount of the community charge through the ballot box unless some illegality is thought to have taken place in the setting of the charge. In the latter case action may be taken by way of a judicial review of the authority's decision-making.

Charge and precept capping

EW Act s 100
part VII   **13.38** The Secretary of State has the power, in specific circumstances, to set a limit to (or cap) the amount of expenditure which a designated authority is undertaking by way of community charge. This power may be used where the amount of expenditure the authority intend to finance from the collection fund is:

☐   excessive in itself; or

☐   in 1990-91 an excessive increase over a notional amount set by the Secretary of State; or

☐   in later years an excessive increase over the previous year.

13.39 Precepting authorities may also be capped where the total of their precepts meets one of the above criteria.

EW Act s 101   **13.40** An authority can only be designated where the amount of its expenditure to be financed by the collection fund is greater than £15 million or a larger amount up to £35 million that the Secretary of State may specify in an order.

EW Act s 100   **13.41** Authorities are designated in accordance with principles established by the Secretary of State. These principles must be the same for:

☐ the same type of authority, e.g. all inner London boroughs, all metropolitan districts, etc.;

☐ those authorities which have or have not been designated in the previous year.

EW Act s 102   **13.42** The Secretary of State writes to the designated authority notifying it of the decision, the principles upon which it is based (para. 13.41) and the lower amount proposed. A designation is invalid if it does not meet these criteria.

13.43 Once designated, an authority or precepting authority has no choice, having had the opportunity to make representations, other than to make a new calculation of its expenditure, or issue a new precept, in line with the Secretary of State's revised figure, if it has been supported by Parliament.

S Act s 22   **13.44** In Scotland the Secretary of State may reduce an authority's
sch 3   community charge where its total estimated expenditure is considered excessive and unreasonable and Parliament agrees. The authority has the opportunity to make representation against any such proposed reductions.

Index

The index refers to paragraph numbers, not page numbers. 'Ch' refers to a chapter number.